SAINTS AND SNAPDRAGONS

Saints and Snapdragons

by LUCILE HASLEY

SHEED & WARD · NEW YORK

Manufactured in the United States of America

FOR MY HUSBAND

ACKNOWLEDGMENTS

With the kind permission of the editors, *Whatever Lola Wants, Lola Gets* and *One (1) Nasturtium* are reprinted from *The Sign; The Pencilling Mama,* from *The Critic; Holiday for Strings,* from *Today;* and *The Case of the Retarded Mrs. Hasley,* from *The Marianist.*

Contents

. . . "The essay is a diversion, a country path, an amble, sometimes a foolishness, a joke and a giant. The article can concern itself with gods or galoshes; but the essay alone can manage both in the same sentence. . . . It can whisper at this corner and roar like a cavalry charge at the next; it can be English horn or diapason; thunder on the left or the sound of a needle dropped on a glass table."

From an essay, *Twig on the Tide,*
by Herbert A. Kenny, in *The Catholic World* (1957).

Essays

Togetherness

Actually, I don't know when a colored magazine ad has given me so much pleasure. There was the slim and smiling young mother, seated in a fan-shaped garden chair, with her smiling family clustered about her: attentively following her long red finger nail as she traced a route on the gayly colored road map spread out in her lap. Underneath, it read:

"Family vacation time is time to relax and enjoy the fun of Togetherness; to strengthen family ties and build happy memories. Mapping out where to go and what to do is half the fun . . . and everybody looks to Mother when it comes to the final decision."

They do?

Carefully and cautiously, I re-inspected those smiling faces that were gathered, with great Togetherness, around the big wheel: Final-Decision-Mother. Mother had obviously just announced where they were going (and how and when and for how long and what stops along the way) and yet I could detect no darkening brows, no tight-lipped tension, on the faces of her dear ones. Neither were there any conversational balloons, issuing from their mouths, to belie those wreathèd smiles.

There was no Daddy balloon saying: "Now see here, Edith! We don't go to San Francisco by way of the Florida Keys . . . you out of your mind or something? This was supposed to be a two-week vacation . . . remember? . . . and we're not going by helicopter, either."

Neither was there a Little Brother balloon: "But, Mom, I told'ja I don't wanna go *anywhere*! I don't wanna miss playing in the Little League! Please, Mom, couldn't I stay home all by myself? I know how to fry an egg and make grape Kool-Ade, and me and Eddie Klotz could sleep out in the backyard in my pup tent. It'd be just neat, Mom. You wouldn't have to worry about a thing, honest."

Neither was Sister dancing up and down in a rage and howling: "But *Mother*! You said . . . you *promised* . . . that this summer we could go to a lake and stay in one spot, not spend all our time cooped up in the dumb car. I want to go to a cottage and bring along Marilyn Shimp and Trudy Applegate! What fun would I have with just my brother? Daddy! Why does Mother have to have *her* way all the time?"

Mothers of the nation, I put it to you squarely: do you, like the Supreme Court, pass down all final decisions? If so, are all your constituents deliriously happy with said decision? Is your family so thoroughly welded together, in one great bond of Togetherness, that you all want to do the same thing at precisely the same time? If so, read no further. I have nothing to offer you. Nothing, that is, except the suggestion that you and your family belong in the Smithsonian museum. Indeed, I can see it already in my mind's eye: your family group in a little alcove, roped off by red velvet, and with a little bronze placard reading: THE DAVIS FAMILY, WHO FOR THE PAST TWENTY YEARS HAS SPENT EVERY SUMMER VACATION IN A FISHING SHACK AT LITTLE BEAR LAKE. NEVER ONCE HAS THERE BEEN A DISSENTING VOTE. NEVER ONCE HAS A DAVIS CHILD ASKED TO BRING ALONG A NEIGHBORHOOD FRIEND. ALL EYES TURN TO MOTHER AND WITH ONLY ONE THOUGHT: "WHAT IS MOTHER'S PLEASURE?"

Bet it'd be the biggest drawing card in the whole museum, with Mrs. Davis (a woman who can't think of anything more pleasurable than a fishing shack) as the chief attraction. Parents might even bring their box lunch and spend the whole day just gazing at the contented Davis family, nudging their children and saying sharply: "Now you look, you kids. You may never see anything like this again in your whole lifetime. My mother once held me up to see President Harding, when he passed through Kokomo, but it was nothing so historic as *this*."

Of course, some young upstart . . . some young rebel

without a cause . . . might just whimper back: "But, Mom, what's the big deal on all this Togetherness stuff? Makes *me* sort of sick to my stomach. I like it the way we do it in *our* family: me going off to Scout camp, Dad taking a fishing trip with Uncle Garvey, you and Sis going off to Atlantic City. . . ."

And I can hear that mother whispering back, nervously: "S-sh! Don't say things like that out *loud*, Son. Outsiders might think we didn't have any Togetherness at *all*."

Son: "And is that a Federal offense, Mom?"

Mother: "Well, not yet, but I understand they're trying to introduce a new bill in Congress. You see, my son, America is founded on the premise that the family that stays together *stays* together; that the family that stays together plays together; that the family that plays together always. . . ."

(Her voice peters out weakly. "Son," she finally manages to whisper, "I'm feeling rather sickish, too. I just remembered that time your father took me quail hunting with him. Come on, let's get out of this place. Look, why don't you scoot out to the ball park for that double-header you wanted to see and I'll catch that Deborah Kerr picture over at the Majestic? We ought to be home by the time Daddy finishes the eighteenth hole, don't you think? But remember, son: we've got to walk out of here *together*, hand in hand. We can separate later, over on Michigan Avenue, when no one is looking. Okay?")

Well, here we see a Mother making all the final decisions, as usual, but this time using her noggin: "Oh! Ye'll tak' the high road and I'll tak' the low road, An' I'll be in Scotland before ye!" Really, a much more sensible tune than the more rowdy *Hail! Hail! The Gang's All Here!* for one's daily theme song.

Personally, I feel that *some* families (mentioning no names) have so much Togetherness throughout the fiscal year that they can jolly well use a little Pull-Us-Apartness. For instance, and this is just a random example, *some* families have a breadwinner who only goes out to win bread at erratic hours (hours that keep shifting every semester, with the new teaching schedules at Notre Dame) and who has a summer's vacation that lasts all summer. Until September 15th, to be exact.

I ask, is this family longing for a few snatched hours Together? Do the children (as in Bob Hope's family) ask: "Mother, who's that strange man shaving in the bathroom? He says he's our Daddy. He says he's just back from Russia."

But, the diehards may point out, what about building happy memories and strengthening family ties in new surroundings? Don't you all *want* to be together when you first see the sun sink over Lake Placid? Mammoth Cave? Salt Lake City?

I am not insensible to the pretty picture this makes: Man and Wife, hand in hand, silhouetted against the sinking sun. Only, I somehow associate it with the honeymoon.

(Hence, one of the smartest moves *this* Man and Wife ever made was to get in a lot of travelling right after the wedding ceremony. We added up the wedding checks received, and melted down some of the silver trays for ready cash, and then said to ourselves: "Shall we buy furniture or shall we go to Mexico while the going is good?" Put that way, the furniture didn't have a chance.) The point is that *after* the honeymoon the picture generally includes several Small Ones (they being the natural result of Togetherness) who, twenty to one, are not remotely interested in the sinking of the sun *anywhere.*

I distinctly remember, for example, one scenic jaunt (post honeymoon) through upper Maine with my two small daughters, twenty-two months apart, en route to Quebec. Here, in gorgeous technicolor, was Nature at its finest: far, far from the man-made wonders of the Asphalt Jungle. We were inhaling the pine-scented air, drinking in the pink and purple sunset, exclaiming over an occasional shy doe when, from the back seat, came daughter Susan's voice. "Wake me up," said this budding Thoreau, "if we hit anything interesting. Like a house."

Or a Howard Johnson with twenty-eight flavors of ice cream. Or a nice nice filling station, such as on the Pennsylvania Turnpike, with lovely violet-ray toilet seats to manipulate up and down. Or a sudden glimpse of H_2O (pond, river, lake, waterfall, creek, irrigation ditch, canal, bayou, swamp, wayside puddle) to trigger off a frantic command:

"STOP! Stop the car quick, Daddy!" (Daddy leaps on the brakes and we skid to a screeching halt, the odor of hot rubber polluting the pine-scented air. WHAT IS WRONG?) Then we hear, "See the water behind those bushes, Daddy? We want to take off our shoes and go wading, Daddy."

Then there was the problem of instilling the rudimentary principles of restaurant and rest-room etiquette. For instance, my children's first encounter with the ancient system of tipping left them absolutely rigid with indignation. If their father was stupid enough to leave perfectly good coins by his plate, their obvious filial duty was to retrieve them. And if they could corral someone else's tip before the waiter spied it, it was just so much of a windfall toward defraying expenses.

Etiquette in gas station rest rooms was even more trying. They would dash in ahead of me and then rush out shouting, for the edification of all passing citizens: "It's okay, Mama! This is a nice one! Tell Daddy he can go ahead and buy the gas." But having learned that rest rooms were free (along, that is, with an honorable purchase of gas), their indignation knew no bounds when they hit their first 10¢ toll fee in a hotel. Jeepers! Waste a whole dime? Before I could grab them, they had crawled under the door and were uttering clucks of encouragement: "Come on, Mama. Keep your head down and you can make it." Everyone in the room, including the maid in attendance, eyed me speculatively. . . .

And how was I to know that Janet would become violently and frequently car sick? Naturally, it wasn't during the secluded and pastoral scenes that she was seized with *mal de mer* but mainly in the thick of traffic. Perhaps, although it's really hard to choose, my most vivid memory of life at its worst was as we were driving past the impressive Château de Frontenac in Quebec. Suddenly, we heard a strangled but all too familiar moan from the back seat. What to do but swerve sharply and erratically up to the curbing? As the misguided doorman, with an elegant and welcoming flourish, opened the back door, Janet leaned out and quietly retched at his feet.

Really, whenever I think of some of those early vacations together, I become so exhausted . . . in retrospect . . . that I have to lie down on the davenport. But no one could say I wasn't being a Togetherness Mother . . . even though, back in those days, the word "Togetherness" wasn't even a gleam in the *McCall's* editor's eye.

Of course, I must admit that things picked up considerably . . . once Janet got over the car sickness . . . but by *that* time my daughters had reached The Athletic Age. True, I was no longer feeding them cod-liver oil and iron tonic, but I was now reaping the golden reward: vigor that never lagged or sagged. ("Come on, Mom! Let's climb the Statue of Liberty again!" "Can we come back to the Bronx Zoo tomorrow?" "Hey, the man at Coney Island said you should bring us back on a Saturday. More fun, more crowds." "Why do you and Daddy keep wasting time by sitting down on the benches?")

I know I'm not exaggerating all this because I have, in my archives, an essay I wrote . . . in the white heat of the moment . . . shortly after returning home. It ends on the plaintive note: "Someday I am going back to New York. I am going alone. I am going on the Pacemaker. And I'm going to see what gay Manhattan looks like after seven-thirty of an evening."

Brave words, bravely executed . . . about ten years later and then only through an Act of God. I mean, you can surely refer to my sudden emergence as a public speaker as an A of G? (Can think of no explanation on natural grounds. Especially when you consider that the only course I ever flunked in my life, the only blot on my scholastic record, was a semester of Public Speaking back in South Bend Central High School.) Anyhow, these A of G lecture requests . . . seeing as how the Hasleys were not a singing unit like the Trapp family . . . were just for *Mother.*

Mother, then, had no choice but to reluctantly swing aboard the Pacemaker, wearing a new outfit, and start learning the ABC of solo travelling: how to pull out the bed in a roomette, be firm with porters ("Nonsense! I can *so* dress in twenty minutes"), whistle for cabs, capture Red Caps, order room service without apologizing for the inconvenience to the hotel cook, approach policemen when lost, interpret train schedules, steam out a dress over the bath-

tub, and . . . above all else . . . to master the nasty business
of tipping every time you turn around. (Solution: Carry
about $50 in quarters in your right coat pocket. This may
make you sag a little to one side but it's preferable, I find,
to plunging into your pocketbook and spilling your lipstick,
compact, reading glasses, and cigarettes all over the sidewalk. Also, do not beat your brains out figuring how much
15% comes to. Make a wild guess and let the chips fall
where they may. We pass through this world but once and
the odds are strongly against your meeting *that* particular
steward again.)

Well, it was naturally pretty rough . . . this basic training
in travelling without a man to pave (and pay) the way and
without any children to point out every bubble fountain . . .
but it had a few minor compensations. Such as Mother
doing and seeing exactly what she felt like doing and seeing.
(I.e.; no Statute of Liberty, no Bronx Zoo, no Coney Island.)
And, once home, Mother did not have to spend another
two weeks emptying suitcases, washing and ironing clothes,
shaking out sand from Coney Island, adroitly disposing of
smuggled souvenirs: menus, salt shakers, paper napkins,
match folders, miniature soap bars, ash trays, and painted
turtles.

So, Mothers, be of good heart. If and when you are ever
forced to go off by yourself . . . be it only for a week-end
attending a Daughters of Isabella convention or a lay retreat
. . . try to remember the key-word: Chin up! It won't prove

too miserably lonely, honest. Nor will your family (although this may come as a rude jolt to you) collapse from malnutrition or sheer stark unhappiness without you. The wheels of living will not grind to a standstill. Rather, you may find yourself greeted by childish trebles: "Hi, Mom. I was elected monitor to the lavatory this week"; or, "Hey, Mom, come look at the neat cave I dug in the back yard." As an afterthought, they may add: "I thought Daddy said you weren't coming home till tomorrow."

The real pay-off, though, will be when your husband says thoughtfully: "Your little vacation must have done you good, dear. You don't look as tired and run-down as usual."

It is my observation that the family unit (providing it isn't based on shifting sands to begin with) can well afford to become unjoined every so often. After all, there is much to be said for the joy of coming together again, after a brief coffee break in all that Togetherness, and having something new to talk about. Nor is there anything like a hotel room to make you gaze around your own lived-in living room with a fresh and unjaded eye.

The main thing, though, is that the family unit (building block of the state, the nerve ganglion of the church, the last repository of Promethean fire) happens to be composed of *individuals,* and these various individuals . . . as they grow up and become more and more individual . . . develop certain pronounced, if quaint, likes and dislikes of their own. Even more curious, the boy individuals seem to enjoy only boy things: baseball, camping, BB guns, wearing old blue jeans and sweat shirts, and living mainly on hamburgers.

Girl individuals, once they reach the stage of putting their hair up in pin curls at least thrice daily, react violently vice versa. Frequently, they're embarrassed to death by the boy individual's sublime contempt for gracious living. (Shades of son Danny, on our first trip to Antoine's in New Orleans, tossing aside the French printed menu and announcing loudly: "What *I* want is a double-malted and a hot dog.")

And neither the boy nor the girl individuals are crazy about trailing through old cathedrals, studying rock formations, seeing famous landmarks, going through antique shops, or rocking on the porch of some secluded lodge. If urged to do *nothing* for any longer than fifteen minutes at a stretch, they ask: "Well, what're we supposed to do? Just sit here and *rot*?"

Mother and Daddy, on the other hand, grow more and more unathletic with the years. You might even say weaker. Sometimes, on vacations, they have barely the strength to walk more than three miles, up and down sand dunes, carrying a lunch basket and a beach umbrella. Sometimes, they even decline to plunge into the cold surf. More and more, they tend to call out from shore: "Yes, dear, we saw you stand on your head! You must have stayed under a good sixty seconds. That's fine, boy . . . keep it up . . . we're watching. Just come out when you start to turn purple."

All of which . . . this variance in tastes and physical

stamina . . . makes Togetherness pretty rugged at times. So when marriage counsellors talk about preserving the family unit (building block of the state, nerve ganglion of the church, last repository of Promethean fire), shouldn't they consider first things first? The thing is, what good are *dead* parents?

What's Your Line?

Even though I don't know the lyrics, I *do* know that the song *When the Saints Go Marching In* is a good rousing tune: the sort that calls for tapping feet, swaying torsos, and clapping hands. I also know that we've had nothing *but* saints . . . forty-four of them, to be precise . . . marching in and out of our house this past month.

This can be pretty strenuous—living and eating with forty-four well-known saints, day in, day out—but now that they've left, and the marching is heard no more, I almost miss them. They *were* a lively if motley crowd . . . all those martyrs, confessors, virgins, and apostles . . . sitting down at the table with us every evening. Nor did we waste time with our usual scintillating small talk ("Catsup, please" . . . "Didn't you salt the potatoes?") but got right down to brass tacks. You might even say we put Mike Wallace to shame: prying into their private lives, demanding their credentials, and even asking them—pointblank!—whether or not they were virgins.

But now that the Holy Cross PTA meeting—featuring the seventh grade in a panel quiz on the saints—has come and gone, life at the Hasleys has simmered down to normal. No longer does Danny follow me around the house, notebook in hand, begging me to turn off the vacuum sweeper and think of a saint. "And don't always pick St. Joseph, Mom. Think of a harder one for me to guess."

(Business of turning off the vacuum sweeper, thinking of a harder one out of the remaining forty-three, and waiting for the inquisition—"Woman? Man? Apostle?"—to begin. It always went swiftly, though, because once he hit a lucky key-word . . . "Born in Lima, Peru?" or "Did she promise to send roses?" . . . the jig was up.)

Well, as I say, the saints have moved out of the house . . . but the odor of sanctity lingers on. Too, it's going to be a long long time before I can pick up a saint's life, over four lines long, and not find it too verbose and long-winded. Oh, I know that Butler's *Lives of the Saints* is supposed to be brief and compact but Butler, compared to son Danny, was a regular chatterbox. Here, for example, are some sketches from my son's "panel quiz" notebook:

St. Matthew:

1. He was a tax collector.
2. Our Lord told him, "Follow me," and he dropped everything and followed him.
3. He was a martyr.

St. Cecilia:

1. She said that she was the bride of Christ.
2. She was put in a hot steam bath heated seven times the regular amount to suffocate.
3. She is the patroness of music.

St. Vincent de Paul:

1. He entered a religious order.
2. He converted his renegade master. (????!!!!)
3. His charity embraced the poor.

St. Francis Xavier:

1. He was a Professor of Philosophy at the University of Paris.
2. He had seemingly no higher aim. (Philosophy profs should *love* this!)
3. St. Ignatius won him to more heavenly thoughts.
4. He wore himself out preaching the gospel to the Far East.

St. John:

1. He was the youngest of the apostles.
2. He was thrown into a caldron of boiling oil and was miraculously preserved.
3. He is called a martyr although he really wasn't.

Now I, myself, would not quibble about St. John's martyrdom . . . boiling oil is good enough for *me* . . . but you can see that, along with the admirable brevity of the sketches,

Danny has the instinct of the true scholar: no hasty accolades for *him*. Can Butler say as much?

But here's the thing. After being put through the wringer on the saints . . . check, check, and double-check . . . I now have a rough idea of what the *families* of the $64,000 contestants go through. Why, I ask, doesn't Hal March at least hand out Cadillacs to those long-suffering relatives . . . those unsung heroes . . . who have labored behind the scenes? It is not easy, living with a high-keyed and distraught contestant. Nor is it easy, once the ordeal is over, to *quit* thinking about the special category that has been consuming one's waking and sleeping hours.

Now it is surely more fruitful to be haunted by saints than, say, the ups and downs of the stock market or hot-rod racing or the works of Charles Dickens. I don't deny this for a minute. Only, I feel that I *can* concentrate better on the spring housecleaning once I get the following little fantasy out of my saint-ridden mind. Nor am I asking first American serial rights on this production. Any time John Daly wants to give his program a shot in the arm, he's perfectly welcome to help himself.

WHAT'S YOUR LINE?

Daly: "And now we come to our special mystery guest. Are your blindfolds all in place, panel?" (Dorothy Kilgallen, Arlene Francis, Ernie Kovacs, and Bennett Cerf all groan and nod their heads.) "Very well, mystery guest, will you sign in . . . PLEASE?"

(The audience, after an audible gasp, breaks into thunderous applause as the name "Francis of Assisi" appears on the blackboard.)

Daly: "And now, for the benefit of our home viewers, we'll let you know exactly what our guest's particular line of work is."

(Monitor flashes on: SAINT)

Daly: "As you know, with our mystery guests, we have just one question apiece and then move on. However, for reasons of my own, *I* will do the answering this evening. I'll just tell you that our guest is a man with a European birthplace. Miss Dorothy, will you start the questioning?"

Dorothy K.: "Well, from all that applause, may I assume you are in the entertainment field?"

Daly (merrily flipping card): "Five down. Mr. Kovacs?"

Kovacs (fiddling with cigar): "Not in show biz, eh? Well, then, I always like to get in my usual question before Dorothy asks if it's bigger than a breadbox. Sir, can your product be *folded?*"

Daly (joining in laughter from audience): "Sorry, Ernie. Miss Arlene?"

Arlene F.: "Well, Sir, are you in a profit-making organization?"

(Mr. Daly and St. Francis go into a huddle. They seem to be arguing a fine point.)

Daly (flipping card): "We have a small disagreement here, panel. Our guest feels his work *is* most profitable, and I must concur, but in our terms of reference the answer must be no. He does not belong to a profit-making organization. Mr. Cerf?"

Bennett C.: "Sir, would it help us any to identify your place of birth? Anyhow, I'm going to take a wild pot-shot. Sir, would you be a famous Hungarian tennis player who arrived in New York last week to raise funds for Radio Free Europe?"

Daly (with false note of rising excitement): "A tennis player, you say? A HUNGARIAN tennis player? No. Miss Dorothy?"

Dorothy: "Sir, would you be self-employed?"

(Again Mr. Daly and St. Francis go into a huddle.)

Daly: "Our guest insists he isn't, that someone *is* over him. However, in our terms of reference . . . and in order not to confuse you, panel . . . I must say that he is, in a fashion, self-employed. Also, that he . . . ah . . . uh . . . deals more in services than with a specific product. Miss Arlene?"

Arlene (fingering her diamond heart necklace): "Might *we* avail ourselves of your services . . . and would we be better off afterwards?"

Daly: "Yes, indeedy. And you, Miss Francis, should feel a special . . . shall I say *kinship*? . . . with our guest. Mr. Kovacs?"

Kovacs: "Brother, I'm lost. Sir, if you're not in the entertainment field, is it possible . . . considering all that applause . . . that you're a powerful figure *behind* the scenes? Maybe a director or an angel that puts up the dough or even a well-known writer?"

Daly: "Well, yes, you can call him a writer . . . and he certainly does work behind the scenes . . . but I can't, in good conscience, refer to him as a capitalist."

Bennett (brightening): "You say, Sir, that you're a writer. Has Random House ever published any of your work?"

Daly (flipping all the cards): "Panel, you're all getting nowhere fast, but I'm going to give you one last clue, just for fun. In the popular mind, our mystery guest is commonly associated with the care and feeding of birds. Care to take a flier, Miss Dorothy?"

Dorothy (smiling whimsically): "I'm afraid I'm not very good in the Audubon department, John. Heavens, all *I* can think of is St. Francis of . . ."

Daly (shouting): "That's it, Miss Dorothy! St. Francis of Assisi in person!"

(Miss Kilgallen, removing her blindfold, just has time to make the sign of the cross before sinking into a dead faint. The other panel members, although remaining upright, look in equal need of an oxygen tent.)

Daly: "Well, St. Francis, you certainly gave our panel a rough time. But I think Miss Dorothy is coming around now . . . yes, her eyelids seem to be twitching. Bennett, you seem to be trying to say something . . . ?"

Bennett (with only a wan attempt at his old aplomb): "Sir . . . I mean, St. Francis . . . I've never given a lecture in

Assisi but I understand your home town is quite noted for
. . . um . . . ah . . ."

Daly (kindly): "Bennett, you and Miss Dorothy had better
step out for a little fresh air. You're both still looking a little
pale around the gills. Audience, St. Francis is making this
unprecedented appearance on behalf of Brotherhood Week.
We had originally asked him for Be-Kind-to-Dumb-Animals
Week but he insisted that brotherhood, among his *un*feath-
ered friends, was really more urgent. And as a special treat
for all of us, he has consented to recite his most famous
prayer. St. Francis?"

St. Francis (upon rising to his feet, we now notice . . . for
the first time . . . a small chickadee nestling in his brown
wool cowl): "I will do so right gladly, John. But first, am I
right in assuming that the country is having a slight reces-
sion? Yes, well, I just wanted to say that Lady Poverty is
an old dear friend of mine and that, really, you shouldn't
go into a senseless panic. She often takes with one hand
and gives with the other, you know. Besides, if you'll pardon
my saying so, *must* you Americans all have two-toned cars
with power steering and white-walled tires? Brother Ass and
I always enjoyed walking . . . sometimes, indeed, we used
to *run* just from the sheer joy of being alive in God's glorious. . . ."

Daly (interrupting St. Francis with the stricken air of a
man who would rather be shot than do so): "Uh . . . I'm
sorry, St. Francis, but they've just flashed me the hurry-up

signal. I know it sounds ridiculous . . . for we've never before
had a saint on *any* network . . . but we *are* followed by a
program called *Harbor Command*. So if you could just give
us that prayer?"

St. Francis (raising his arms in a simple and graceful gesture that seems to embrace all creation): "Lord, make me
an instrument of Thy peace; where there is hatred, let me
sow love; where there is injury, pardon; where there is doubt,
faith; where there is despair, hope; where there is darkness,
light; and where there is sadness, joy. . . ."

There is a split-second of stunned silence, followed by
Mr. Daly saying hurriedly: "And this is your host, John
Daly, saying goodnight now for *What's . . . YOUR . . .
Line*???"

Monkey On My Back

It seems rather a pity that my brain, unlike the late Albert Einstein's, will never end up in a glass jar for medical observation. My friends have been telling me for years that I . . . well, you know how friends are? Always thinking you're another genius or something? Even so, I honestly can't begin to tell you how often my friends have told me: "Lucile, you ought to have your head examined."

Those are their precise words, I swear it. And even allowing for a certain amount of over-enthusiasm on their part, I can't help feeling that their opinion ought to count for at least something. Don't you?

For myself, of course, it really doesn't matter. It has never been a life-long ambition of mine . . . I mean, ending up in a glass jar at Princeton . . . and the *personal* satisfaction I might get out of it strikes me as being practically nil. However, it just might settle, even though posthumously, an argument that I've been having with my husband.

He has always clung to the pretty notion that his wife, despite her Gracie Allen exterior, was a reasonably intelligent woman—and I, of course, have always backed him up in this. That's what wives are for: a solid support at all times. So *that* isn't our argument at all. I certainly *am* an intelligent woman, providing you don't count the areas where I don't even try: mathematics, economics, politics, sports, agriculture, astronomy, bee culture, mechanical engineering, etcetera.

It still leaves a lot of room (the world being so full of a number of things, I'm sure we should all be as happy as kings) for happy intellectual hunting.

For instance, my particular forte happens to be working the crossword puzzles in the Chicago *Tribune*. A most worthy pursuit. Only, I have long since passed the early stage of "addiction" (I use quotes because the expression belongs to my husband): that innocent period when you can take it or leave it. Just the sight of a puzzle . . . all those delicious little white squares pleading to be filled in . . . and my fingers start twitching, quite uncontrollably, for a pencil.

Nor am I one of those people who can toss the paper aside with an exasperated: "Oh, the heck with it! Who *cares* what a Greenland settlement is, anyway?" *I* care. I care most passionately. That unfinished little corner, thwarted by a four-letter word meaning Greenland settlement, is a challenge that *must* be met before the sun sinks. (Or, preferably, before noon.)

As I recall, this all started last April when my son got a Chicago *Tribune* paper route. We figured it would be great character training for him (getting up in the grey still watches of the morning and getting the papers all delivered by 7:30 A.M.) but no one reckoned on what it would do to *my* character. "You understand," I said sternly, "that this is *your* responsibility? That your father isn't going to pile out of bed and deliver the papers for you just because it's raining? That you're to be quiet as a mouse and not disturb the rest of the household?"

Yes, he understood. Then, about the second morning, I heard a low keening sound from the living room. Stealing downstairs in my bathrobe, I discovered the young Horatio Alger on his knees, trying to fold papers on the living room floor, and weeping bitterly. The clock on the desk said 7 A.M. "These dumb ol' papers just won't fold," he moaned piteously. "Call the dumb ol' agency and say I'm quitting."

Quit on the second day? Heavens, this could establish a *pattern* of quitting that might warp his character for keeps. Besides, there was the initial outlay, advanced by his father, for the money-changer, paper punch, and rubber bands. Would Horatio have abandoned ship?

Quickly, Mother sank to her knees and started bending the bulky papers, slipping a green rubber band around each miniature bale of wood pulp, and heaving them into the gaping canvas bag. "Quit sniffling," I hissed. "We don't want your father to hear us. Just *fold*."

By the end of April, my character-building was coming along just fine. We were meeting that morning deadline with nary a slip along the line and my son had *almost* enough quarters stashed away in a quart Mason jar for a down payment on a Daisy rifle. Too, I had developed a certain affinity by now for the Chicago *Tribune*, in spite of my strong Democrat leanings, and occasionally . . . after Danny had staggered out with his load . . . would pick up a frayed copy (torn by that fiendish wire clamping the whole batch together) that was unfit for a paying customer. I, you understand, was not a paying customer. Just part of the unpaid help.

Then one morning as I sleepily perused a copy, not quite so mangled as its predecessors, I discovered the crossword puzzle: completely intact, and nestling cozily at the bottom of an inside page. (As I later discovered, you not only had to hunt for words unknown to Webster, but you had to hunt first for the puzzle itself. All part of the fun.)

Carelessly, I reached for a pencil. It might help kill the next half-hour, waiting for smiling Dave Garroway to bring me the latest national disasters and the weather report from San Antonio.

Only, Garroway got lost in the shuffle that morning. Three hours later, still crouched over the puzzle, I was saying to myself: "This is *ridiculous*. I used to get a straight A in English. What has *happened* to my brain over the years?"

After that, I was a sitting duck when my son said plaintively: "Mom, even if you *are* a Democrat, couldn't you break down and subscribe? It only costs 45¢ a week and you'd have a puzzle to work *every morning.*"

Yes. Well, even the alcoholic starts out with a daily little snifter. He never intends it to get out of hand . . . no, not *him* . . . and what harm in a little something to warm his veins?

At first, I used to call out to my husband: "Hey, this is right down your alley. Who was the wife of Geraint? Four letters starting with E." This worked for awhile (all that "Surely, *you'll* know this one" sweet talk), but he eventually reached the point of saying, "Flattery will get you nowhere. Look it up for yourself in the dictionary. It'll do you more good that way."

Next, he began saying: "Come to think of it, what good *is* this doing you, anyhow?"

Next, he began saying (rather nervously) as he left for a ten o'clock class: "By the way, dear, what are you planing to do today? Anything special lined up?" It was rather like that TV commercial for Playtex gloves: a tender male voice querying, "Tell me, dear. What are your lovely hands going to do today?" I suspect . . . else why the unprecedented interest in my agenda? . . . he was afraid that *my* lovely hands were going to do nothing but wield a grubby little pencil, flip the pages of *Webster's New World Dictionary,* and let the rest of the world drift by.

This is patently ridiculous. My lovely hands have never

yet failed to have the supper at least *started* by 5:30. And I still observe many of the social amenities. I mean, I have never yet turned down an important luncheon invitation by saying, "Gee, thanks, but I'd rather stay home and finish my crossword puzzle."

So why the complaints?

Well, for one thing, he doesn't seem to care for the absent-minded way I kiss him goodbye in the morning, murmuring tenderly: "Did you know that sapid means savory? Isn't that amazing? I mean, sapid *sounds* like vapid. Even sappy. But I checked it both ways and it seems to be right. And did you know . . . boy, this will really kill you . . . that agnate means 'related on father's side'? I always thought an agnate was a marble."

Now wouldn't you think, honestly, that an English professor—of all people—would be absolutely delighted with a wife like this? Not only adding to her own rich vocabulary but freely, and most generously, sharing her wealth of information with others?

Instead, he is . . . by now . . . going around like a man who is bleeding internally. Too, he keeps pestering me with deep and probing scientific questions like: "*How* can an intelligent woman like you squander so much valuable time? If we counted up all the lost woman hours, we'd find you could have written another book by now." He even goes on to predict that my brain, weighed down by all this excess and useless information, is going to start crumbling at the

edges. Whereupon I say (although only that glass jar exam-
ination would offer conclusive evidence) that this is sheer
nonsense. I say: "Nonsense. Look at a fruit cake. It doesn't
collapse. In fact, the more nuts and bits of candied citron
and orange peel you throw in, the *better*."

But just how, he asks, do I plan on utilizing such little bits
as e-n-t-e (heraldry, grafted) or s-t-a (music as written) or
r-o-m (gypsy) or e-r-i-a (Japanese silkworm)? Am I plan-
ning on weaving these into my social conversation, and being
the life of the party, or what? Surely, not dumping them into
my essays?

It's a nice question, only I wish he hadn't asked it. All I
can point out is that my mother used to collect used Christmas wrappings, bits of twine, and assorted buttons. Hadn't
they on occasion (say, every seven years) come in right
handy? Someday, I might even visit Japan and then where
would I be . . . not knowing a common household word like
eria?

All good answers, only none of them work.

What I can't explain (for only another crossword puzzle
devotee would understand) is the simple and childlike joy
I derive from what I call The Light Breaking Through the
Clouds. Such as trying to decipher a definition like: "It
marches in January." Clearly, this is nothing for Webster
to handle. You're on your own and . . . what four-letter word
does march in January? Well, I know the answer but I'm
not telling. If you lie awake tonight, tossing and tossing, it

just *may* give you a rough idea of the insidious fascination that we puzzle hounds know only too well.

Also, I have discovered that a crossword puzzle is almost as revealing as a Rorschach test. What's so different from giving your first spontaneous impression of an ink blot and the first instinctive word that leaps to your mind as a synonym? For instance, I recently hit the definition: "Jumping-off place. " *My* mind immediately conjured up an electric chair, the Foreign Legion, Lover's Leap, and a dangling noose. So I really became rather alarmed about my mental health when I finally discovered that a jumping-off place was simply a springboard. I mean, why couldn't *my* mind have conjured up Esther Williams executing a swan dive into her backyard pool? Have I been watching *Climax!* too much?

Also, I find that my Catholicism often gets in the way. What is a four-letter word, starting with M, meaning "Queen of Heaven"? Look it up for yourself, it'll do you more good. Only, I *can* tell you . . . after bitter and incredulous hours of research . . . that it is *not* Mary.

But now . . . if you'll please excuse me? . . . I have a little unfinished business of my own.

"Let's see. I've just got this one little old corner to clear up . . . forty-six down . . . oh, *no*. Not that 'Babylonian hero' again! I've looked it up a million times and always forget . . . well, I know it starts with an E. Etay, maybe? No, that's the Greenland settlement. Eria? No, that's the silkworm, bless its little heart. Besides, this is *five* letters. Steady now, Hasley. You'll get it in time if you just don't panic. But maybe if I went out and did the breakfast dishes, it might come to me? No, that's walking out on the problem. Business before pleasure, I always say. I'll give myself just ten more minutes . . . E . . . E . . . I'VE GOT IT! ETANA! Now, the rest is a cinch because I *know* that an ait is a river island and that ser is an Indian measure of currency. . . ."

Boy, do I ever feel like a new woman! And now that my homework is finished, I can take care of the piddling chores . . . awaiting my lovely hands . . . with a crystal-clear conscience.

P. S. Indeed, I now feel so refreshed . . . and so kindly toward the world . . . that I've decided to tell you what marches in January. A *dime.* Get it? The March of Dimes. But I'm not giving in completely: the "Queen of Heaven" is still yours.

Please Don't Take Thursday Off!

The cast for this play originally called for 50,000 cherubim, 875,000 seraphim, and 9,375,000 angels. However, owing to technical difficulties in assemblying such a large cast, I have since reduced the characters to two guardian angels.

I have also made one other slight concession. That is, the two angels were to have appeared in their natural state . . . i.e., pure spirit . . . but this was found to be unsatisfactory when the play opened in Philadelphia. The audience demanded their money back at the box-office. Hence, the play now calls for two very visible and very virile-looking young men . . . preferably along the Rock Hudson or Farley Granger type . . . wearing traditional angel costumes: wings, togas, sandals, etc. Flaming swords, if they can be managed, also add a nice touch. (Incidentally, our costume designer found that this traditional garb is more effective than a stream-lined version. In tights, the angels just looked like Superman. And while angels can, on occasion, assume the ordinary appearance of man, we found that a three-button business suit was not too dazzling. Better stick to the wings.)

The scene opens with the two angels resting companionably on a single cumulus cloud, their flaming swords tossed carelessly aside. It is a Thursday, their day off.

Incidentally, we also had a little trouble with *this* in Philadelphia: the theologians protesting that guardian angels maintain a constant vigilance over man, with no time off. Not even a coffee break. However, we just wouldn't have any play at *all* if we removed this little discrepancy. Besides, I'd just like to see the theologians write a strictly theological play about angels and see how far *they* got. Bet they wouldn't even get as far as Philadelphia.

1st Guardian Angel (idly sifting a piece of cloud through his fingers): "Hmm, wonder if people would worry if they knew they were on their own today."

2nd Guardian Angel (gloomily): "Fat chance. Why, most of them don't even believe we exist. *We*, the big brothers of mankind, with our angelic mission to protect, direct, inspire, comfort, encourage, etcetera! Yet the only time they ever mention us is when some young idiot, driving his hotrod at eighty-five miles an hour, just misses breaking his neck or something. Then they all say, 'Gosh, man, your guardian angel must've been working overtime,' but it doesn't mean anything, you know. Just a stock phrase. No one *really* thanks us."

1st G. A. (raising himself up on one elbow in some concern): "If you ask me, angel, you really need Thursdays off. Your color hasn't been at all good lately, not to mention your so-called angelic disposition. Is your Mary Flanigan, down in Fort Wayne, Indiana, still going steady with that no-good Zip Morrison? But don't tell me! Let's not talk shop on our free day. Let's just relax and drift a little, huh? Say, this cloud rides as easy as a new DeSoto. . . ."

2nd G. A. (refusing to smile): "Well, maybe I have been a little edgy lately, but I *still* don't feel right about taking Thursdays off. That's strictly a man idea . . . this shortened week business . . . and I'll bet you didn't clear it with Head-quarters, either. Frankly, I think *your* charge . . . that Detroit industrialist, Mr. Bloomingsdale . . . is influencing you more than you're influencing him."

1st G. A. (whistling): "That's a pretty accusation, I must say. But go on. What else is eating you, angel?"

2nd G. A. (somewhat abashed): "I'm sorry, I guess I shouldn't have said that. But look, angel, *why* don't people believe in us any more? They can't see electrons and atoms, either. Besides, we're so much nicer, don't you think? I mean, I should think they'd *want* to believe in us . . . instead of scoffing at the idea . . . when heaven knows they grab at everything else for comfort and assurance: positive think-ing, yogi, tranquillizers, vodka on the rocks, etc. Gee, do you remember the good old days . . . back in the Middle Ages, I think it was . . . when people even got excited about us? Stood on street corners, speculating as to how many angels could dance on the head of a pin? Now they're hopping up and down with excitement, and even laying bets, as to who'll be first to reach the moon. Tell me . . . angel to angel . . . just *why* we fell into obscurity. Is a man-made satellite so much more spectacular than we are? We're not even confined to an orbit. . . ."

1st G. A. (soberly): "Well, if you *insist* on spoiling my Thursday, I suppose that the answer (remember, now, I haven't the power to read a man's mind!) is that men don't believe in us because they don't much believe in themselves. I mean, they can't quite believe in their own dignity and worth; can't believe that they are . . . in the Divine Scheme . . . entitled to such individual, and angelic, attention. Really, I think that's the catch. Not the fact that they can't see us. After all, their minds are practically aflame nowadays . . . what with all this outer space excitement . . . and they're believing, and accepting, lots of things they never even imagined before."

2nd G. A. (stubbornly): "Yes, but God has *said* we exist. We're all over the Bible . . . and in pretty stellar roles, if I do say so: the Annunciation being (to my mind) just about the nicest to remember. My, wasn't Our Lady's acceptance speech magnificent? And we were in *both* gardens . . . Eden and Gethsemani . . . and at the Birth and at the Tomb and . . . well, it just leaves me speechless. Men even sing *our* song every Christmas—'Peace on earth, good will to men,' but do we ever get any credit for the lyrics? But I'm not

thinking so much about *our* dismissal from man's minds . . .
honest, I'm not . . . as about the reflection on *Him*. Even if
man can't prove, by reason, that there's even *one* angel in
existence, doesn't His word carry any weight?"

1st G. A.: "Come, come, let's not go into *that*. Not on a
Thursday. Anyhow, the word 'angel' hasn't been completely
dropped from the English language. Little kids still make
what they call 'angel wings' in the snow; they still call the
financial backers on Broadway angels; they still refer to St.
Thomas (who wrote so nicely about us) as the 'Angelic
Doctor.' And then there are so many little things, too: like
that face powder called 'Angel-Spun' and that brittle glassy
stuff called 'Angel Hair' that they put on Christmas trees.
Ah . . . come on, angel. Things aren't so bad. We might still
stage a comeback someday. Besides, God didn't create us
just to act as baby-sitters for Man. We both praise and reflect
His Glory . . . remember? . . . and we're not supposed, as
angels, to let men disturb us unduly. We're supposed to be
happy, happy, happy. St. Thomas *says* so."

2nd G. A. (abashed): "I know. Sometimes, I feel just plain
unworthy of my wings. But dadrat it all, these human beings
can get under your skin. Now you take my Mary Flanigan
. . . you know, the girl in Fort Wayne? I've done all right
by that girl, if I do say so as shouldn't, since the moment
she was born. Why, I even made her mother change her
mind, practically at the baptismal font, about what to call
the poor kid. Remember the case? They *were* going to call

her Candy. Imagine if she later married a man named Barr! Only, now I'm worrying, all over again, about this Zip Morrison character she's got in tow."

1st G. A. (rolling over on his back): "Send her a three-cent stamp. Let her write in to Ann Landers for advice. After all, you know what they sometimes say down on earth: 'You did your best; the angels can do no more.'"

2nd G. A. (coldly): "Fun-ny, fun-ny. Listen, I've got a real problem on my hands, I tell you, and my Mary is pretty special. That Mary is a real responsibility . . . I just *can't* let her dash her foot against a stone at this point . . . but the trouble, if you can imagine it, is that she's almost *too* good. *Too* angelic. In fact, she keeps forgetting she's just a human being and tries to take over *my* job. Thinks she can reform that young lout, Zip, once they're married: one of the most frequent and misguided notions known to women! And, of course, Zip plays it for all it's worth—even to calling her 'Angel.' He keeps feeding her this line: 'So what if I *can't* keep a job, drink too much, am on parole from the State School, and quit the Church and the eighth grade at the same time? I love you, angel, and that's the big thing, that's what counts. With you beside me, angel, I'd become a new man.' Sometimes he even sings to her (he hasn't a bad tenor) to clinch the deal. Songs like *All the Way* . . . and *I'd Climb the Highest Mountain. . . .*"

1st G. A.: "Stop. I'm feeling slightly sick to my stomach. You know, you're *completely* ruining my day off. . . ."

2nd G. A. (leaping to his feet and grabbing his flaming sword): "Well, what do you think it's doing to me? I tell you, I can't stand it another minute! Thursday or no Thursday, I've got to check on that girl." (Dives from cloud.)

1st G. A. (peering over the edge): "Hey, come back! You're forgetting your angelic nature! St. Thomas says we angels *can't* feel anxiety!"

Voice floating back: "Yeah? They say the same thing about Our Lady! Go ask *her* to explain the right terminology. . . . I've got my hands full . . . I've . . ."

1st G. A. (sighing): "He's right, of course. We're *not* entitled to Thursday off." (Rises, grabs flaming sword, strikes a pose, and repeats—aloud—the Angelic Oath.) "God hath given His angels charge over thee, to keep thee in all thy ways. In their hands they shall bear thee up, lest thou dash thy foot against a stone." (Dives off cloud, in general direction of Detroit.)

Holiday for Strings

The present popularity of mood music albums . . . *Beautiful Music To Love By, Ballads for a Smoke-Filled Room, Hillbilly Music for People Who Can't Stand Hillbilly Music, Music While Taking a Bubble Bath*, etcetera . . . leads me to believe that Edward R. Murrow is right. Our country *is* in a weakened condition.

I mean, it stands to reason that by now there must be millions and millions of people who can no longer function (take baths, make love, study, shampoo their hair, telephone, fall asleep, wake up, face smoke-filled rooms) without a musical accompaniment. Somehow, this background music seems to serve as both a stimulant and a pain-killer although here and there, let it be noted, you find a person who reacts vice versa. (These people, generally parents in their forties, sometimes say things like this: "Listen, you! I dare you to play that Little Richard record *just once more*!!" Or, "The rule in this house, as long as we're still

supporting you, is no music before 6 A.M. *Understand?*")
However, we must remember that every society, since early
cave days, has had its quota of recalcitrant members. People
who drag their heels.

It is also interesting to note that this universal (well,
almost universal) demand for music, and dependence there-
on, also extends to the animal kingdom. That is, I understand that what started out as an experiment—piping music
into the barn to make the cows give more milk, the hens lay
more eggs—is now a barnyard *must.* I also understand that
the cows and the hens, like people in their forties, become
moody and hostile when exposed to the good strong beat of
the electric guitar or Bongo drums. Respond nicely, though,
to Perry Como.

Anyhow, I presume this same principle (music maketh
more milk, more eggs) explains why my supermarket fur-
nishes canned music, from 9 A.M. until quitting time, for its
shoppers. Under the hypnotic influence of, say, the score
from *My Fair Lady,* you forget your original and modest
shopping list (hamburger, graham crackers, and Tide) and
dreamily strip the shelves. Glassware, potted plants, tooth
paste, frozen guinea hens, home permanents, *everything.*
Then, when you and your brimming cart finally reach the
cashier, the music helps deaden the pain and the shock of
it all.

Also, I should report that I recently had a tooth extracted
and woke up, in the anteroom, to the sweetest music this

side of heaven. It was really one of the happiest moments of my life, spitting blood in the little white basin and listening to the violin arrangement, but I never *did* learn the name of that particular music album. (The nurse was too busy, holding my head and handing me Kleenex, to pay any attention to my mumbled query.) All I have to go on, as a lead, is that it was a lower bicuspid on the left side that was pulled. So, I naturally suppose . . . wouldn't you? . . . that the album was called something like *Holiday for Strings After Losing a Lower Left Bicuspid That Couldn't Possibly Be Saved*.

Funny, you just never seem to run across simple little titles like *Nola* nowadays. It's reassuring to know, though, that there are special recordings to see us through *all* Life's little exigencies: from the delivery room right down to the funeral parlor.

This, then, is the American way of life. And while I'm quite willing to string along with it, I can't help thinking of an item I recently saw in the newspapers. A seventy-five-year-old man in New York, nabbed by the police for possessing narcotics, protested to the judge: "But I've been taking heroin for the last fifty-six years. Never felt better."

Yes, but what happens when the supply is withdrawn?

After all, there are a few isolated occasions, such as travelling in an upper berth, where it is awkward to smuggle along one's record player. What, then, is our music addict to *do*? The silence is unbearable. The prospect of being alone with his own thoughts only heightens the pain. And the blessed benison of sleep, that might knock him out of his misery, is quite impossible without his nightly music capsule.

Moreover, to add to his mounting panic, he is accustomed to being told—by the latest survey out of Chicago—just *what* music he should be listening to and enjoying with social impunity. Hence, the poor man can't even hum or whistle a few bars of music, on his own hook, as an emergency measure. Indeed, in his terror, he may not even be able to recall the ten top tunes of *last* week's survey.

In brief, this man needs help.

Now, my idea is to bring out special albums of "mood reading" that might tide people over until they can get back to their record players or radios. However, the public must be wooed gently and I think . . . at least right in the beginning . . . I should call my product: "The Music of Words, Without Electric Guitar Accompaniment." Or do you think "Silent Music for the Inner Man" might be better? Neither of them makes much sense but I feel, quite strongly, that I should get the word "music" in somehow. Later on, after the idea catches fire, I could come right out and say what I mean: "Selected Mood Reading for Special Occasions." If careful in my publicity releases, I wouldn't need to use the word "books" at all.

To date, I have prepared the following tentative albums:

A.　"What To Read When You Feel Like a Good Cry for No Good Reason at All." (Carefully selected excerpts from

Our Town, Long Day's Journey into Night, Heartbreak House. This is for women who are refreshed and invigorated by the cleansing power of tears.)

B. "Reading for Raising One's Blood Pressure." (This is for men who have been on tranquillizers too long but whose systems can't tolerate the new miracle stimulant, ZXPL. Here, I thought the most effective approach would be to collect the various editorials—dealing with the right-to-work laws, foreign aid, Dulles, separation of Church and state, fluoridation, etc.—that have enraged the greatest number of readers throughout the country.)

C. "What To Read While in Bed with a Head Cold and Feeling Mighty Sorry for Yourself." (Selections from the lives of the saints. Special emphasis on St. Joan at the stake, St. Lawrence on the spit, St. Catherine on the torture wheel. This reading will not improve the mucus drainage from your sinuses but it might possibly shame you into shutting up about it.)

D. "Reading for Guests Who Have Overstayed Their Welcome." (Here, my idea is not to drive the guest away by brutal measures . . . such as insisting he read, and finish, *By Love Possessed* . . . but by this new hidden persuader method. Any sensitive guest, especially if you've already packed his bags and placed them out in the vestibule, should think twice as he scans the index: *Return of the Native, A Passage to India, Grand Hotel, The Need for Roots,* and *Look Homeward, Angel.*)

E. "Reading for People Who Have Seen the Movie but Never Read the Book." (Genesis, Exodus, Leviticus, Deuteronomy, etc. Would also include colored pictures of Charlton Heston (Moses) and Anne Baxter (Egyptian love interest) so DeMille fans won't feel *too* lost.)

F. "Reading To Lull You Asleep Practically Anywhere." (Not to be confused with reading to bore you into an unhealthy stupor. I mean reading that leaves you pleasantly exhausted; gives you the vicarious feeling that you've *earned* a good night's sleep after a day spent tilling the earth, chopping down timber, baling hay, mending fences, etc. Hence, my winning vote . . . from a wide range of low-keyed regional literature . . . goes to Elizabeth Madox Roberts' *The Time of Man.* Incidentally, I've *tried* this. Works lots better than hot Ovaltine.)

G. "Reading To Take the Place of a Stomach Pump." (For people who have accidentally swallowed poison and need a quick emetic. Excerpts from *Peyton Place, The Naked and the Dead,* etc. After retching has taken place, this is to be followed by soothing excerpts from *The Fresh and Open Sky, The Friendly Persuasion,* and *The Reed of God.* Keep on reading until the doctor arrives.)

H. "What To Read While Travelling." (This would include four different sections, depending on whether you are travelling by train, plane, boat, or Greyhound. Since it's all under one cover, though, I *must* ask you to use the honor system. For instance, I will not be responsible if some nervous soul, on her first trans-Atlantic flight, dips into the wrong section and reads the hair-raising *God Is My Co-Pilot*. Likewise, I would not recommend *The Wayward Bus* for those going by Greyhound or *The Sinking of the Titanic* for those aboard ship. All selections may be thoroughly enjoyed, however, if you stick to your right category. The enjoyment will mainly stem from the cozy feeling: "Boy! Am I ever glad that *I'm* going the safe way.")

Incidentally, I would like to point out another fine feature of my reading album for travellers: the simple and chaste, yet tastefully designed, tooled leather cover. Of course, if you want to be cheap about this thing, you *can* grab up a paperback novel in the train station for only two-bits. Nothing to stop you. Nothing, that is, if you don't mind sauntering into the club car with a half-naked woman in a pink chemise. Remember, too, that you can hardly explain to your smirking fellow passengers: "See here, this book is *really* about electronics. The cover has nothing to do with it."

Now I'll be the first to admit that this project of mine still has a few wrinkles to be ironed out. Still, I think the time has come to kick it around in the open and sound out public reaction. Or as Madison Avenue would say, it's time to get out of the high grass onto the green. Or, let's blow feathers around the room. Or, let's run it up on the rack and look underneath. Or, let's wring it out and see what drips from it. Or, let's run the flag up the pole and see who starts saluting.

Well? Any salutes? Any drippings?

But first, in order to sharpen our wits, maybe we'd better have a little background music. I understand there's a new album, just released, called *Music To Help You Think While Wringing It Out To See What Drips* with Crazy Mitch at the snare drums. They say the beat is terrific. They say it makes you concentrate like anything.

On First Dipping Into Mr. Sheed

Mr. Frank Sheed has perhaps caused me more mental anguish than any other living Catholic author, and this, when I stop to think about it, covers a lot of territory. Nevertheless, I feel that Mr. Sheed has rightfully earned this distinction, hand over fist, and I am only sorry that my Anguish Award is a little late in the day. Every Catholic in the United States—or at least every Catholic worth his salt —probably read *Theology and Sanity* ages ago, and just why there haven't been more yelps of pain from those salty Catholics, I wouldn't know. It just goes to show, I guess, that some people *like* to suffer.

Well, I suffered at the hands of Mr. Sheed and didn't like it and no one is going to talk me out of it. Whether or not I benefited by that suffering is entirely beside the point. The fact that *Theology and Sanity* is as painless as possible, considering its painful contents, is equally beside the point. The fact that I read the book with my own little free will, with no one pressing a bayonet to my back, is even more beside the point.

The immediate point, my friends, is that I suffered. Would *you* be feeling so good if you discovered, after only one chapter of Mr. Sheed, that you had an enlarged and inflamed imagination, a non-functioning sense of reality, a high resistance to logic, and a very low mental count? That's the sort of thing that should be broken to a man gently and in a physician's office.

Of course, Mr. Sheed didn't come right out and say, in so many words, that I had a low mental count, but I caught on to this myself—especially when I hit that fourth chapter: "The Mind Works on Infinity." I wouldn't know just whose "working" mind Mr. Sheed was referring to but it couldn't possibly have been mine. I blacked out early in the game. I remember thinking, just before I lost consciousness, that it was certainly a dirty shame that I hadn't been born back in the fifth century. I understand that back in the fifth century people treated the village idiots with a certain reverence; asked for their blessings; regarded it as good luck to have them underfoot.

Mr. Sheed, however, seems to have scant reverence for idiots. *He* seems to think it's our own idiotic fault for letting our intellectual muscles get so flabby.

Well, a person can't go through something like this—being called everything from flabby on down the line—and remain quiet about it. Fortunately for posterity, I have not remained quiet. I have, in my old 1952 files, a very fascinating exchange of letters between the author and myself: letters that I believe will, in time, be ranked alongside those of St. Paul and Timothy. I realize that it is customary to wait until a person is dead before publishing his personal correspondence but, in this instance, I would like to dispense with the usual formalities. The last time I saw Mr. Sheed he looked disgustingly healthy and . . . well, anyhow, here are the letters.

Dear Mr. Sheed:

In a recent issue of the *New Yorker*, I came across this poignant little item: "A six-year-old New Jersey lad who has just learned to count into the hundreds asked his mother what the very last number is—'the very very last number.' She told him that there isn't any last number, that as far as you go there are always more numbers ahead of you, and was complimenting herself on having neatly slipped the conception of infinity into his consciousness when she noticed that he was quietly crying."

I, Mr. Sheed, am not the type that weeps quietly when confronted with the staggering concept of infinity. Hence I am taking this opportunity to say that I've just started studying *Theology and Sanity* on the Notre Dame campus and that there are moments when I definitely loathe you. My finite brain is ready to *bust* trying to follow you through time, space, essence, being, activity and immutability, and God knows what all. And, worst of all, my lovely imagination—my stock in trade—is whimpering like a forlorn orphan: unloved, unwanted, unclaimed. You, Mr. Sheed, say that imagination clutters up straight thinking and *certainly* has no place in the field of theology. This, to me, is practically a death sentence. I need my imagination just as I need my lungs.

Formerly I was very happy in my ignorance and even managed to cash in on it. (See *Reproachfully Yours.*) Moreover, there was a certain admirable purity about my ignorance (it was so whole, so complete, so infinite) and now you've even wrecked that. I feel as Eve must have felt when she suddenly realized, after the Fall, that she was only wearing a fig leaf.

All this, you say, is part of the painful process known as facing the world of reality; stripping oneself of formerly cherished but 100% wrong conceptions. I have only one question to ask, Mr. Sheed. What are you, personally, prepared to do about the feeble minds that, once stripped, can't clothe themselves again? You had better think of an answer, fast. What you are doing to my mind practically amounts to highway robbery.

For instance, you have robbed me of the pretty notion that God's happiness depends pretty much on *my* day-to-day actions. Perhaps I have always known better, in my subconscious, but it's pretty shattering when you force me to stop and think about it. I *want* God to be offended or rejoiced at what I, Lucile, do. I don't want God just to *be*. The way things stand now, I can't even say my morning offering . . . "Oh, my God . . . not *offend* you this day . . . " without feeling silly. Yet if God can't

feel offended, why do so many of our prayers imply
that He can? I suppose that the correct answer hinges
on the metaphysical conception of *time* and I cannot
get *time* through my thick skull. Even if I did, it would
take the punch out of everything.

Look what you're doing to one of your own promising
authors! If it doesn't make your heart bleed, you have
no heart.

Yet wait a minute, Mr. Sheed. What about these
apparitions where Christ (as appearing to St. Margaret
Mary) and Our Lady (as at Fatima) appear bowed
down with suffering? They can no longer suffer in
heaven and so where's the catch? Would Christ and
Mary mislead people just to stir up zeal and contrition?

To date, the only thing you've managed to drive home
successfully is that I am utter nothingness and am held
in existence from moment to moment. Thanking you
for nothing, I remain

> Sincerely yours,
> "Utter Nothingness"
> (Formerly Lucile Hasley)

Dear Utter Nothingness:

It's not fair. I didn't heckle you about your book. I
didn't loathe you for it or threaten to disintegrate you
for it. There should be some mutuality in these matters.
But note:

So your finite mind is ready to bust? So is mine. One
gets used to it. The explosion that doesn't quite take
place is, after a while, companionable. So your imagina-

tion is whimpering? What a little fool imagination is. For its comfort, read it some sententious word about how much more fun imagination has when the intellect it serves knows its own business. And what about the minds that, once stripped, can't clothe themselves again? Any mind that has the energy to strip itself will have the energy to clothe itself again. At a certain level of feebleness, the mind cannot do either. If it can do one, it can do the other. So take heart, little sister.

Isn't all this nice and snappy? But about the apparitions of Our Lady and Christ bowed down with suffering, no snappy answer will work. Two things I'm sure of: (1) They are now in total bliss . . . the brightest phrase scripture has about heaven is "there shall be no tears." (2) They are not pretending to cry just to get us crying, while laughing like anything out of our range of vision. They are not a pair of hams. After these two things, nothing is sure. We do know, though, that Our Lady and Our Lord do have a reaction to the sin and sorrow of this world; it does not diminish their total bliss, but it is a real reaction all the same. The recipient of the vision may catch something of this reaction, and the nearest we can get to it is a feeling of tears in the air.

At this level, the questions that arise in the mind of an intelligent reader cannot, strictly speaking, be "answered"; one can talk about them and catch glimpses of light as one talks, but that's all. Let's talk about them sometime.

Yours ever,
Frank Sheed

Dear Mr. Sheed:

Thank you for your helpful letter. I thank you in particular for the implication, even though unfounded, that I am an intelligent reader. A fascinated but moronic reader would be more like it.

By the way, you may be interested to know how you are handled on the N. D. campus. In this new theological project for faculty members and wives, Sheed can be had on three levels: like getting low-grade, regular, or Ethyl gas at a filling station.

1. Source course, under Father Sheedy. This is for the intellectual but snoopy faculty people who are interested in tracking down Sheed statements to Moses or the Council of Florence and such stuff.

2. *Theology and Sanity*, under Father Miltner, for those who are well-grounded in philosophy.

3. *Theology and Sanity*, under Father Murphy, for the simple-minded. I guess I told you before I am in Father Murphy's class?

After these sessions, held every Sunday evening, the sheep and the goats all gather together in the faculty parlors for strong hot coffee. Brandy (with or without a St. Bernard) is what we really need.

I would like to say in passing that I recently made the mistake of picking up another of your books: *Translations of the Little Flower*. I was actually very much taken with this job and found myself, for the first time, gracefully swallowing all that "Jesus, let me be your rubber ball" stuff. But look! The theme of the book is that Thérèse keeps wanting to *console* Christ and there is only one little footnote to put the reader right: "The saint, of course, fully understands that Christ no longer needs consoling." Who reads footnotes, pray? Besides, there is just that one little footnote versus 999 pages of consoling the sorrowful Christ. This does not strike me as a very logical way for you, of all logical people, to handle the situation. Also, what about this common expression that God *craves* souls? Isn't *crave* a pretty strong term for a non-created spirit who is infinite, utterly self-sufficient, utterly blissful, etc., etc.?

Sincerely yours,
"Utter Nothingness"

Dear Utter Nothingness:

Your question interests me considerably. The plain truth is that St. Thérèse seems to have had no instruction worth mentioning on the Blessed Trinity. When she thinks of God, it is almost invariably of God-Made-Man. (This, I think, is largely what vitiates Graham Greene's *Heart of the Matter*. Scobie is all the time thinking of a God whose face he can smack.) If you say that the height of sanctity Thérèse reached seems like a good argument for knowing as little about the Trinity as she did, I can only say that she would probably have been a saint if she had read nothing but the Koran. This, of course, would be an answer given in haste, which I should probably be much embarrassed to defend. Anyhow, I am sure that when she speaks of God as craving souls, she is thinking of Christ; but when she speaks of "consoling" Christ, what does she mean? It may be that she is making use of the fact that just as all the sins ever to be committed played their part in

Christ's suffering during His Passion, so all the acts of
love ever to be directed towards Him were a consola-
tion at that time. Or it may be that she has in mind the
thing I tried to convey in my last letter: namely, that
Christ—here and now in heaven—has *some* reaction to
the sin and sorrow of the world. It is not suffering but
it is something. She no more knew what it is in the
psychology of One who had the Beatific Vision than I
do, and she may have thought that to "console" was
man's best reaction to that unfathomable reaction in
Christ.

> Yours ever,
> Frank Sheed

Dear Mr. Sheed:
Thank you for your helpful letter. I simply cannot
understand, however, how God. . . .

But why go on? The above exchange will give you a rough
idea as to what I've been going through, thanks to Mr. Frank
Sheed, and how I deeply appreciate G. B. Shaw's comment:
"When I learn something, I feel as if I had lost something."
I would not, however, like to leave my readers (probably
crying in their beer by now) with the impression that Mr.
Sheed, despite the mental anguish he has caused me, is a
theological monster with two heads. I know for a fact that
Mr. Sheed has only one head. The last time I saw him I took
particular care to notice.

I have only one head, too. All I can say for the flabby little thing is that, in tackling *Theology and Sanity,* it showed a certain gallant if foolhardy courage.

But isn't it nice, when you stop and think about it, to belong to a Church that isn't scared of questions? That doesn't even throw you in the Bastille for questions that *appear* to be almost heretical? Oddly enough, I have noticed that priests far prefer this challenging approach in a prospective convert to an apathetic and passive "Okay, Father, if you say so, Father. Now am I ready to be baptized?"

And how very nice to ask a question and *not* be met with a pious rolling of the eyes and the solemn incantation: "This is a very great Mystery." (Translated, this means: "Shut up. Move on.") Yet even the mysteries that *are* real mysteries (and this, I'm afraid, would include God Himself) can afford to be contemplated, can't they? A mystery is a mystery. Not an unreality. And you can at least, under the Church's guidance, come up with something a little more profound than Jane Russell's classic remark: "I love God! When you get to know Him, He's a living doll!"

Again, isn't it nice to ask a question and *not* be met with: "But what does it *matter*? Why bother your pretty little head? The answer can't *possibly* have any bearing on your daily routine."

Or, the even more frustrating: "Well, this calls for an individual interpretation. What does the Bible say to *you*? You see, it's like poetry: each man digs out what he can."

Really, all things considered . . . and I'm *almost* ready to forgive Mr. Sheed at this point . . . it *is* rather nice to belong to a Church that has a question-and-answer period after the lecture. Nor does curiosity necessarily kill the cat. Not, that is, if the cat is lapping up the cream out of the *right* saucer.

Laughing With Leacock (Ha)

Up until last Friday, around 7:30 P.M., I had always thought of Stephen Leacock . . . the late professor-humorist from Canada . . . as a very very funny man. I might even have said, had you encouraged me, that I didn't see how a college professor *could* be so funny. That is, intentionally funny.

I might also have said, prior to last Friday, that my favorite essay—in his *Laugh With Leacock*[1] collection—was the one entitled "Letters To The New Rulers Of The World," with letter #3 (To a Plumber) the funniest of the lot. It started out, this missive to the plumber, in Leacock's usual suave and courteous manner:

> My very dear Sir: It is now four hours since you have been sitting under the sink in my kitchen, smoking. You have turned off the water in the basement of my house and you have made the space under the sink dry and

[1] New York, Dodd, 1930.

comfortable and you are sitting there. I understand that you are waiting for the return of your fellow plumber who has gone away to bring back a bigger wrench. . . .

Well, it went on in this detached vein . . . all very amusing with its low-keyed humor . . . and really left me fractured. Of course, it might not appeal to just everyone . . . there are always the oafs who prefer pratfalls and custard pies . . . but it was certainly *my* dish of tea.

Then, last Friday night, my own kitchen drain backed up on me and I quit laughing with Leacock: he of the warped sense of humor and no delicate sensibilities whatsoever.

Well, I won't go into all the ugly details of that kitchen drain . . . none of them being remotely amusing . . . but I found myself on Sunday morning (and right during the 12:15 Mass, if you must know) composing a letter to *my* plumber. Only, unlike Leacock, I wasn't complaining . . . in whimsical vein . . . about his presence under my sink. My problem was what you might call a little more basic.

Mr. Ralph Schultz
Schultz Everready Plumbing Service
610 Elm Street

My very dear Sir:
   It is now thirty-eight hours since I first appealed to you for help and, with each passing hour, my longing to see you grows more intense. It's true that I am a mar-

ried woman, and should perhaps show more emotional restraint, but *when* are you going to keep your tryst with me? Your voice sounds ever so nice over the phone . . . personality plus! . . . but I'm dying to see you in person. You know what I mean, Ralph? Yet when your wife answered the phone early this morning (and I'm sorry about getting her out of bed), I somehow got the impression that you had lost interest in me. *Permanently* lost interest. Or are you provoked because I asked you (during our last chat together) to at least *guess* at an estimate? Sorry. Guess I spoke out of turn.

Anyhow, my dirty dishes are mounting toward the ceiling . . . the pots and pans are all over the floor (did I mention that the dirty drain water, no doubt breeding malaria flies by now, has inundated all the shelves under the sink?) . . . and it's really very awkward trying to cook without water. Oh, we're not exactly starving . . . I found a box of Wheaties this morning that were still dry . . . but I always like coffee to keep up my strength. Besides, that's what the Red Cross always serves to disaster victims.

Truly, I hate to have you see my kitchen (I have a pink and pewter grey color scheme that's normally rather effective) in this condition. I also hate to ask you to come out on a Sunday afternoon, even at double rates, because I'll bet you like watching all those cultural programs on TV: *Omnibus, Meet the Press,* etc.? Still, I promise to make things as pleasant as possible for you. Do you like potato chips and beer?

Cordially,
Mrs. Louis Hasley

P. S. I *think* my husband has quit trying to fix the drain by himself (that's how the washer on the drain trap got broken in the first place, you know) but I can't guarantee anything. You'd better hurry, Ralph.

Well, the letter wasn't as suave as Leacock's (*he* would never have fawned on Ralph in so crude a fashion) but I wasn't feeling at my most suavish. Anyway, it was the best I could manage under the circumstances. I mean, the Mass going on and everything offered a certain amount of distraction: fishing around for my 25¢ seat collection, standing for the Gospel, etc. But just as I decided to buckle down to my prayers (comforting myself with Thomas Merton's soothing: "The man who has never had distractions doesn't know how to pray"), I suddenly thought of some *more* letters to be taken care of. You know how a thing like that sort of snowballs along, once you get an *idée fixe*? And the *idée* was getting more and more *fixe* that maybe Ralph would *never* show up. The thing is, you have to prepare for such exigencies; can't let things just slide along any which way.

So by the time the *"Ite, missa est"* wafted out over the congregation, I had composed the following . . . and really quite imperative . . . letters for immediate delivery:

Letter #2

Dear Sister Aquinas:

As a special favor, could Danny eat in the school

cafeteria this week? I know you banished him for a month (after that unfortunate chocolate milk episode with little Ruth Mencheski), but could you please reconsider this verdict? We seem to be having a little trouble with the plumbing in the kitchen.

Incidentally, Danny says he didn't really *throw* the chocolate milk at the Mencheski girl, that it just slipped. Even Leopold got a second chance!

Sincerely,
Mrs. Louis Hasley

Letter #3

Rev. Theodore Hesburgh
President of Notre Dame
Notre Dame, Indiana

Dear Father:

I know you're a very busy man (running the University, serving on Eisenhower's Civil Rights Committee, Papal delegate to the International Atomic Energy Commission, etc.), but I know, too, that you're never too busy for a *real* problem. You see, Father, my husband and I are waiting for the plumber to arrive and don't dare leave the house. So could you possibly find someone else to take over my husband's classes for this coming week? Of course, if Ralph (that's the plumber) hasn't arrived by Easter vacation, we would then have to work out a more permanent arrangement for a substitute.

Sincerely,
Lucile Hasley (Mrs. Louis)

P. S. Perhaps I should explain just *why* my husband must be here when the plumber arrives. Well, I not only want this Ralph Schultz to explain a few facts of life to him but I also think Louis should be on hand to help me clean up the mess. Don't you? Also, Father, I think that this . . . in a certain sense . . . is also Notre Dame's responsibility. That is, my husband graduated from N. D., magna cum laude, but was never *once* offered any courses in plumbing. Surely, this is not in accordance with your earnest desire to turn out "the whole man"?

Letter #4

Dear Ellie:

How nice to hear from you! And how *very* nice of you to invite us to spend a week at your cottage next August. We'd love to accept . . . and naturally *want* to plan on it . . . but I hesitate to make a definite commitment right now. That is, we are having a little family crisis at the moment . . . Ha! Ha! don't we all? . . . and things are rather up in the air. Or, to be more precise, all over the kitchen floor. But I'll keep my fingers crossed!

Love,
Lucile

Letter #5

Dear Ann Landers:

I've never before written to an agony column like this . . . and maybe you'll just laugh at my little problem . . . but it's very real to me, Ann. What I want to know is, what do you think of a fix-it-yourself husband who will absolutely *wreck* the place before calling in professional help? Ann, does this mean he is sick, sick, sick . . . or cheap, cheap, cheap . . . or just what? (*He'd* say he's poor, poor, poor.)

Mainly, Ann, I think it's a matter of Principle with him. I mean, he has always deeply admired Thoreau (you know, the bloke who settled down at Walden Pond with only the basic necessities, like a hatchet?) and he deplores the complexities of the Mechanical Age. He actually has a very even disposition, Ann, but something seems to snap inside of him when our appliances go haywire. He has a theory that just about everything . . . refrigerators, washers, driers, toasters, TV sets, etcetera . . . are diabolically geared to collapse one week after the guarantee expires. Is there anything to this, Ann? Well, the other night it was our kitchen drain. I said, "Don't you dare touch a *thing*! Call the plumber!" and then *he* said: "Don't lose your head! Don't you know what plumbers charge, woman? I'll just use Drano and the plunger and then tape this little thingamajig together with bicycle tape."

Ann, you just can't imagine the *mess* he wound up with. I finally went to bed around 11 o'clock, without speaking, and I haven't done much talking since, either. Mostly, I just chat with Ralph Schultz (that's the plumber who is considering coming out someday) and his wife.

My husband reads your column every night and thinks you're a pretty sharp cookie. So why not give him one of those "Wake up and smell the coffee" sizzlers you do so well? He won't listen to me. Just says I don't have the true Walden Pond spirit. What do you say, Ann?

SICK OF IT ALL

P. S. Our Church frowns on divorce. You'll have to come up with something less drastic. Maybe I could just run off with the plumber? We haven't yet met but when we do . . . well, I have a feeling we're going to click like a Geiger needle. It may prove bigger than we are.

Anchors Aweigh!

"By now I understood that Lolly was one of those women who work off emotions in a ritual of domestic science. In a crisis, some women light candles to a saint, and some light the oven and bake whatever is the hardest thing to make."
A *Growing Wonder*, by Hildegarde Dolson[1]

Just to show you the sort of Leaping Lena mind I have, I really thought . . . for a split second . . . that Miss Dolson's sentence was going to end "and some women light the oven and stick their heads in."

Immediately afterwards, of course, I felt good and ashamed of myself. Women, in a crisis, *would* be more likely to bake the hardest thing they knew of . . . say, a Baked Alaska? . . . rather than turn on the gas and commit suicide. Most women, in a crisis, have courage to spare. Moreover, the life instinct in females is especially strong (Mother Nature has made a point of seeing to this) even though women

[1] New York, Random House, 1957.

do tend to say things like: "I'm so happy/miserable/embarrassed/humiliated/hungry/exhausted/furious that I could SIMPLY DIE!" Only, they seldom do. (See insurance statistics re: the likelihood of women outliving the men who have made them so happy, miserable, embarrassed, humiliated, hungry, exhausted, furious.)

But as to which is *better* . . . lighting candles or lighting ovens in an emotional crisis . . . I can only say that I'm in favor of both. They make a nice team. Perhaps the candle-lighting should come first, thus enlisting help from above, and then the oven-lighting could help ease the tension of waiting . . . and simmering . . . until relief (natural or supernatural) sets in.

Certainly, the ritual of domestic science is one of the most ancient methods known to women, of all lands and of all ages, for keeping the show on the road. In fact, I now find myself understanding . . . rather late in the day . . . just *why* my mother used to announce, out of a clear blue sky: "I think I'll clean out the attic!" or "Somehow, I just *feel* like making doughnuts today." It never made any sense to me, truthfully, even though I couldn't help admiring the authority in her voice: somewhat like a weathered sea captain, checking the wind and barometer, and then announcing: "Today we sail! Anchors aweigh!"

Anyhow, I daresay that the early cave woman let off a lot of tension by chewing animal pelts (a housewifely chore, preparatory to garment making); that our American squaw ground out a lot of emotion along *with* the corn; and that the Yugoslavian peasant, trampling barefoot on the grapes, tramped out a lot more than grape juice. I also daresay that without this emotional release, things would have been a lot rougher on their menfolk.

Bringing this down to 1958 push-button America, I myself recently conducted a poll . . . among the members of my St. Anne Discussion Club . . . as to what *they* did in an emotional crisis. What took the place of chewing pelts, grinding corn, trampling on grapes? Well, it proved fairly interesting but not too conclusive: none of them having the same sort of crisis in mind. After all, there is a vast discrepancy between a burnt-to-a-crisp supper (and a burnt-to-a-crisp wife, thanks to a delinquent husband held up at Casey's Tap Room) and the emotional tension of waiting outside an operating room.

Finally I, always the life of the party, specified that it should be a sudden crisis . . . of serious import . . . and with the helpless anguish of *not knowing* the key factor. Such as receiving a long-distance phone call reporting a plane crash, but stating they weren't sure as yet whether your husband was aboard. That, of course, was just a rough example . . . maybe I could have done better with a little time? . . . but I suppose the Mike Todd crash was still fresh in my mind. Anyhow, I said, they could draw their own parallels. Oh, and one last thing . . . this anguished waiting should last at least twenty-four hours.

Surely, I urged them, they could think of *some* similar siege of tension? A child lying in a coma . . . waiting for X-Ray results . . . waking up at 5:00 A.M. and finding your daughter still out on the town? Yes, they sure could. (Up to this time, incidentally, they'd been in the best of spirits. Now, thanks to me, you could almost *see* their facial muscles tightening. What did Pearl Mesta, the hostess with the mostes', have that I didn't have to liven up an evening? Still, it was all in the name of research.)

What, then, I urged, had they done to preserve their sanity at the time? One and all reported that prayer instinctively came first: very edifying, but not too surprising considering the group. No one reported that they had gone out to buy a new hat, drowned themselves in TV, or started reading *War and Peace* as a distraction. Rather, the vast majority reported that they . . . to relieve tension . . . liked to go out in the back yard and yank weeds. (One woman, indeed, said she once grabbed up an axe and chopped down a dead tree.) A popular runner-up activity was scrubbing the kitchen floor on their hands and knees. (Using a mop wasn't the same thing at all!) And no one, but no one, had even *thought* of baking chocolate eclairs or Baked Alaska. It simply wasn't violent enough.

So where does this leave us? Nowhere in particular, I'm afraid. I am not even, as a matter of fact, going to hand over my findings to the Kinsey Research Institute. I suspect that they've already established the fact that the gentler sex isn't always so gentle; that the portrait of Whistler's Mother, sitting and rocking with folded hands, isn't quite representative of the entire female race. (All of which reminds me of a rather appropriate joke. One day Whistler came home and found his mother scrubbing the floor. "Why, Mother," he exclaimed, "you're off your rocker!")

Maybe so, but you and I know *why* she was scrubbing the floor, don't we? Just letting off steam.

But enough oven-lighting. Anchors aweigh! It's candle-lighting time.

What I *am* interested in is exploring a woman's inner resources when it comes to recovering from some dreadful wound: the loss of a child or a husband; accepting and living with the irrevocable realization that your new-born infant is a Mongoloid; the stunned disbelief that mental illness could strike *your* family; having a son or a daughter who has married outside the Church; watching a beloved parent die by inches before your eyes or, equally painful, sink into doddering senility.

None of this is very much fun. (I know. I speak with a fair amount of authority.) Nor can *anything*—lighting candles, lighting ovens, swallowing tranquillizers, yanking weeds, scrubbing floors, taking a trip around the world—numb the initial pain. Before the healing process starts (and there's no rushing this necessary waiting period) you can only live with this pain, on a take-one-day-at-a-time schedule, and know that you're *not alone.*

This is indeed a world where hurtful things happen, but your particular pain is not *unique.* Millions of people have gone through this same ordeal . . . *are* going through it right this very minute . . . and yet somehow they manage to pick up the pieces. It's rather like the incredible miracle of all nature: is it *possible* that the stiff, brown, dead-looking clump of twigs in the corner of your yard will ever again be a flowering lilac bush? Yes. You see it happen, every spring, with your very own eyes.

This is God's truth: Good Friday followed by Easter.

Only, I suggest that you do not go up to the bereaved mother in the funeral home and blithely assure her that "Time heals all wounds." Also, you could afford to skip that bit about it being God's Holy Will. (The unspoken question, next following, would be, "And you WANT to do God's Holy Will, don't you?" What this woman wants is her child back. She is not prepared, at the moment, to make any more commitments.) The best thing you can do for this grieving Rachel who will not be comforted is just to press her hand, put your arm around her. If your tears mingle, no great harm done. There is much to be said for the comforting sense of *touch*; the unspoken acknowledgment of pain that is well-nigh unsupportable. The human touch spells tenderness; unlike words, it cannot misfire in its message.

I am thinking now of the parish priest who administered the Last Rites to my eighty-year-old mother. Was she scared and was she lonely? She was. Throwing the liturgy out the window, that blessed priest sat down on the edge of her bed, gathered her up in his arms like a lost child, and said: "Honey, haven't we been friends for a long long time? Why are you afraid of me *now?* Why, look, honey, I administered Last Rites to another good friend of mine only a month ago. Yesterday—guess what!—yesterday I saw her downtown buying a new hat!"

My mother brightened.

And while none of the above monologue, I'm sure, can be found in the official prayers of the Church (the official part . . . and beautiful it is . . . came later), I would not be averse to priests putting their arms around their stricken sheep more often! (Maybe the Church could insert, in red ink, directions for same in the liturgy? *Hold hand. Pat shoulder. Stroke brow.*) Again, I am reminded of this same priest at a graveyard scene: throwing his arm around the grieving widow (my *violently* anti-Catholic aunt) and leading her tenderly back to the car. I'm sure that none of the rest of the ceremony . . . the sprinkling of holy water, the mumbo-jumbo of Latin phrases, the mumbled Hail Marys . . . meant anything to her. But that arm around her shoulder? Yes, she could understand *that.*

"What a nice young priest," she kept saying in later years. "What a comforting man he was."

By the same token, I'm not averse to family doctors who display a little empathy. In brief, I'm not averse to empathy in *anyone*.

But, you may think, is there not something rather shameful . . . you might even say unchristian . . . in allowing yourself to suffer (to the point where your chest actually aches) for and with other people? Isn't it a sign of weakness, emotional bathos, to know such empathy? And isn't it hard on *you*?

"The healthy person," say the Overstreets in *The Mind Alive*,[2] "does not feel less pain and sorrow than his less sound fellow, but more. His security lies not in the avoidance of suffering but in the fact that he *can emotionally afford to feel it.*"

We are not here speaking of the little old ladies who enjoy weeping at weddings and funerals (of parties unknown) or the women who enjoy nothing more than a four-hankie special at the neighborhood Bijou. I am speaking of the real pain, in a very real world, that can eat into our very vitals: either for ourselves or for those very close to us. Or even, for all of that, people we have never known.

I know for a fact that many women say a quick Hail Mary whenever an ambulance whizzes by; a child is reported lost or kidnapped over the radio; or the evening paper carries a story that stings their hearts.

Is this feminine *weakness*? I think not. These are the

[2] Harry and Bonaro Overstreet; New York, Norton, 1954.

healthy women. The unhealthy woman is so wrapped up in her *own* ancient sorrows, so busy keeping the wound alive and throbbing, that she has nothing left over for others.

We all, say the Overstreets, have touchy spots, emotional bruises, wounds that have never quite healed; places where the scar tissue still aches in bad weather. But the revealing clue to one's emotional (and, I might add, spiritual) good health, is the ability to bounce back: to acknowledge one's responsibility to a situation in which *others* also have a stake.

But just *how* do you fight your way back, *how* recuperate? I, myself, am in favor of drawing an Iron Curtain over hurtful things that can't possibly be helped. Now, the psychiatrists say that nothing is ever forgotten; that everything sinks into one's subconscious; and that these sunken items . . . years later . . . can raise the very devil. I still say: Let them sink anyway. They can't possibly cause any more mischief, fifteen years hence, than if they're kept alive in the conscious mind by *brooding*. The one thing essential, it seems to me, is to take a long last good look at the item to be sunk . . . recognize the reality of it, with no kidding oneself . . . and then bury it and be on your way.

"All things have their season, and in their times all things pass under heaven. A time to be born and a time to die. A time to plant, and a time to pluck that which is planted. A time to kill, and a time to heal. A time to destroy and a time to build. A time to weep, and a time to laugh. A time to mourn, and a time to dance."

Once, during a very bleak period of my life (a non-laughing and non-dancing time), I wrote to Sheed and Ward and offered my services as a guinea pig: much as a "lifer" at San Quentin offering to be inoculated by some deadly serum in the interest of science. Wrote I: "If you would like to try out any of your new spiritual books on me, I'd be the perfect guinea pig. If the spiritual uplift doesn't *nauseate* me, you can be sure it has real merit. Has passed the acid test."

The thing about spiritual reading, especially when one is feeling bruised and battered, is that it must ring true to *your* ears. The imprimatur, in the front of the book, may be perfectly valid BUT is that author talking your language? Does he know how you're feeling? Does he know you want no nonsense about rushing out to embrace suffering with open arms? That you can stand just so much, and no more, of the heroics of St. Rose of Lima?

What you really want is the assurance he's *with* you, that author, and isn't just spinning out golden phrases for his own amazement. You want the same down-to-earth realism that C. S. Lewis offers: "All arguments in justification of suffering provoke bitter resentment against the author. You would like to know how I behave when I am experiencing pain, not writing books about it. You need not guess, for I will tell you. I am a great coward. But what is that to the purpose? When I think of pain—of anxiety that gnaws like fire and loneliness that spreads out like a desert, and the heartbreaking routine of monotonous misery, or again of dull aches that blacken our whole landscape or sudden nauseating pains that knock a man's heart out at one blow, it quite o'ercrows my spirit. If I knew any way of escape I would crawl through sewers to find it. But what is the good of telling you about my feelings? You know them already; they are the same as yours. I am not arguing that pain is not painful. Pain hurts. That is what the word means. I am only trying to show that the old Christian doctrine of being made perfect through suffering is not incredible. To prove it palatable is beyond my design."[3]

Now that's the sort of writing that makes you, if you're addicted to marginal notes, grab up a pencil and inscribe some pungent and telling comment such as "How true" or "You're telling me?" or a heavily-underlined "*Yes!*"

The author has struck home; you're now ready to listen to him. Only, it's really quite a nuisance . . . at the height of some emotional crisis . . . to go plowing through spiritual books, hunting desperately for an author on *your* particular wave length. The smart thing, really, is to have a time-tested circle of authors who are *already* old friends of yours. For myself, I know that the poems of Charles Péguy (*God Speaks*), Caryll Houselander's *Reed of God,* and Francis de Sales' *Introduction to the Devout Life* . . . to name but a

[3] *The Problem of Pain:* New York, Macmillan, 1944.

few of the old faithfuls . . . have done yeoman service over the years.

But let us back to the lighting of candles in time of an emotional crisis. I myself am not addicted to candle-lighting (a pretty gesture . . . leaving one's lighted taper glowing in a darkened church to keep your prayers company . . . only one that never occurs to me) but I suppose . . . in a larger sense . . . that *anything* that makes God seem nearer and closer could be classed under candle-lighting. And the Church, incidentally, has quite an assortment of candles. . . .

But do you know what I found out, first hand, to be the most valuable thing of all to sustain one in suffering? I will tell you. A painfully acquired background of solid Christian Doctrine. I say "painfully acquired" because it is not easy to study, really study, the nature of God and the attributes of God and man's relationship to Him. (See my essay "On First Dipping into Mr. Sheed"!) But it all pays off, it really does, when the going gets rough. It means you won't waste time, flailing the air, and letting out time-honored screams of *"How* can a good, kind God permit . . ." or *"What* did I do that God should so punish me?" or *"Why* should this happen to me, who have labored long in the vineyard?" Etcetera, etcetera.

In brief, the suffering still hurts . . . make no mistake about that . . . but you are spared *bitterness*. Hence, the healing period can start sooner than if you had to start from scratch, as it were, and claw your way up to the surface. And while you certainly don't know why the Lord has handed you this cross (and in this world probably never will), your faith in a providential pattern does not crash, or even sag unduly, under the strain. You've prepared yourself ahead of time, see? God is still God. Not a sudden monster.

And now all (all!) that remains is to wait, with as much patience and fortitude as you can scrape together, for that famous healing process to start. "Teach us to care and not to care," writes T. S. Eliot in his poem *Ash-Wednesday*. "Teach us to sit still."[4]

Those brown, stiff, dead-looking twigs, standing out in the March slush, will again bear lilacs.

[4] New York, Harcourt, 1930.

As the Twig is Bent

If some anthropologist, in distant centuries, should ever unearth my high school memory book, I can only wish him *bon voyage* in reconstructing a certain "Lu" Hardman. The poor man won't even have a jawbone to study: just pages and pages of drivel, yielding such gems as:

> Skin-em-aree! Skin-em-aree!
> Skin-em-arinkie, dinkie, dye;
> Flippity-flop! Who's on top?
> Central! Central! Central!

> Alla ga-nee ga-nac ga-nac
> Alla ga-nee ga-nac ga-nac
> Hoo-rah! Hoo-rah!
> Central!

Possibly, this may greatly excite the anthropologist . . .
unearthing a strange new language of such unearthly
beauty . . . but where will it lead him? Will the strong
rhythmic beat and poetic cadenza lead him to believe it a
primitive love call? That "Central" was perhaps the name
of the maiden being wooed? Or *will* he deduce that it was
simply a tremendous cry, splitting the throats of the "Hoosier
Hysteria" fans, as some lanky youth dunked a leather ball
through an iron hoop?

And will he know that the Hoosier maidens . . . clad in
middie blouses, flowing ties, and baggy serge bloomers . . .
also dropped leather balls through iron hoops? I hope so.
Otherwise, what would he make of the newspaper clippings
(that I can scarcely believe with my *own* eyes) stating that
Captain Lucile Hardman, at guard, put up an exceedingly
favorable exhibition of defensive play for the Sophomores?

This may throw him badly off the scent: leaping to the
conclusion that Captain Hardman . . . a born athlete . . .
continued to reap fresh laurels well into her middle years.
Or, that she at *least* kept in trim. Little will he know that
the Captain (although still strongly defensive in many
areas) will only walk to the grocery store, two blocks away,
in a dire emergency. Such as a broken car axle or something.

And will that anthropologist, as he pores over the memory
book, recognize WIT when he sees it? Such as an occasional
blank page labeled: "Out at present. Have a seat. Will return

later." And will he roll on the ground, clutching his sides in helpless mirth, as he comes across this item from the school paper?

Jean K.: "Are you letting your hair grow?"
Lucile H.: "Well, I don't see how I can stop it."

And while the following lyric, written by my geometry teacher, isn't supposed to be humorous, will our man know when *not* to laugh? To me, it's even lovelier than Keats's *Ode to a Nightingale:*

Lucile
Dainty little face
Form of airy grace
Eyes so very blue
Heart that's good and true
Ways so very real
　　(Matchless appeal)
This is Lucile.

The thing is, that geometry teacher *couldn't* have written the same thing in everyone's book. Look at the way "real" and "appeal" and "Lucile" all rhyme. And I'm not ashamed to admit that the line "form of airy grace" can actually make the tears come to my eyes. It really can. It's so sort of nostalgic.

So far, if all goes well, our anthropologist will have established that this "Lu" Hardman had a form of airy grace (not muscle-bound, despite her athletic prowess) and a tremendously mature wit for one only sixteen. But what about her appreciation of the classics? That'll be a snap. On page 19 we find:

Books Read during First Semester

The Sheik . . . . E. M. Hull
Three Weeks . . . . Elinor Glyn
Tish . . . . Mary Roberts Rinehart
Red Pepper Burns . . . . Grace Richmond
Story of Julia Page . . . . Kathleen Norris
Laurel of Stonystream . . ? ? ?

Nor did she neglect The Theater. Aside from the vaudeville shows every Saturday afternoon, at the local Orpheum, we find evidence that she and her sidekicks . . . by skipping lunches . . . scraped up enough money for occasional jaunts to Chicago. Faded programs show by the marginal comments (*"Terrific!"* . . . *"Heavenly!"* . . . *"Out of this World!"*) that Lu Hardman could appreciate even heavy fare:

No, No, Nanette!
Applesauce
Stepping Stones (Fred Stone)
Lollipop (Ada May)

There is also evidence that "Lu" Hardman, along with her fondness for musical comedy, had a sensitive appreciation of classical music. Real long-hair stuff. A yellowed clipping from the local newspaper carries this report: "Miss Alice White, accompanied by Miss Lucile Hardman at the piano, sang 'Gypsy Love Song,' 'The World Is Waiting for the Sunrise,' and 'A Smile Will Go a Long, Long Way' over the local radio station. They scored heavily with the receiving audience scattered from coast to coast."

I'm inclined to believe that "scattered" was hardly the word. But if any residents out on the West coast *do* remember this broadcast, and remember it with pleasure, I'd be terribly happy to hear from them. At any rate, our anthropologist will search in vain for any other reference to Miss Hardman at the piano. It would seem, after this one brief flash in the pan, that Miss Hardman went back to her ukelele. That she, and another talented classmate, did a tap dance *while* playing their ukes ("Five Foot Two, Eyes of Blue") on Stunt Nite: scoring heavily with the receiving audience seated on the bleachers. Only why, I wonder, didn't they get to use the encore ("Mississippi Mud") that they'd also worked up?

It would seem that here was talent . . . oh, talent in abundance . . . but that the world just wasn't ready for it. Later, a more persevering young lady . . . Helen Kane by name . . . was to rock the world with "Boop-Boop-a-Doop" and "Button Up Your Overcoat." But that's show biz for you: some hit the skids, some rise to the top.

But what (and here we're coming into the home stretch) about our "Lu" Hardman's character? Does the memory book indicate how the twig, during these green years, is bending? Yes, indeed. On every side we find stout character references like: "In my wall of friendship, I'll always think of you as a brick." Or, "May our friendship be like the ocean which never runs dry. Yours till the kitchen sinks. Love, Flo." (Flo? Flo *who*? Can this be that horrid Florence Kreighbaum who sat behind me in Latin II? The one I couldn't *stand*? But no matter. The main thing is that she prized our friendship; didn't want it to ever run dry.)

But what I hope the anthropologist *won't* miss is the character testimonial written by one Miss Dobbins, my English IV teacher: "If anyone wants to know, I can certify that a task given to Lucile means a task accomplished. Perseverance along this line, mingled with your love of fun, and people will make such a woman as I could wish you to be."

She was teaching me *English?* Boy, that last sentence really loses me . . . "people will make such a woman" . . . but I suppose that's why I, today, lose so many of *my* readers? As the twig is bent. . . .

But what we must look for (as in my writing) is the glint of gold in the muddy syntax. Clearly, the nugget of gold in this instance is this: "A task given to Lucile means a task accomplished." I mean, it's practically enough to get me into West Point. Yet while it reads very well, very well indeed, there's something about it . . . can't quite put my finger on it . . . that is mildly disturbing. As I search my soul, I'm inclined to think it's one of those half-truths that don't bear too close a scrutiny.

True, I've never missed (although the near missing would sound like *The Perils of Pauline*) an editorial deadline or a speaking engagement in my life. This latter has included, incidentally, two floods . . . that virtually submerged the New York Central Lines . . . and one electrical storm, over the Allegheny mountains, that almost submerged *me*. I even wrote a farewell letter to my family . . . I really did . . . as the lightning flashed, the plane dipped and sank, and all creation groaned in travail. I knew, of course, I'd never get a chance to mail the letter . . . but maybe a half-charred fragment would be found, later on, on the jagged mountainside?

It was a frightful experience, frightful, but I . . . good

trooper that I am . . . made a swift recovery. It only took me four years to muster the courage once again to set foot in a plane.

All this testifies, I hope, to the strong the-show-must-go-on streak in my moral fibre that the discerning Miss Dobbins had noted years earlier. Still, I suspect that if a Roving Reporter were to go around asking people, "Pardon me, Sir, but would you say that a task given to Lucile means a task accomplished?" he might come up with some interesting variations.

For instance, my husband's version would probably go: "A task given to Lucile means a task accomplished . . . *eventually*. Only why does she wait until August to moth-spray our winter clothes? Why are my new pajamas, that I gave her three months ago to be shortened, still lying on top of the dresser?"

My publishers might tell our Roving Reporter: "Yes, a task given to Lucile means a task accomplished . . . but *how*?"

My pastor might come up with a querulous: "Hmm, how do you get her to take on a task in the first place?"

Mainly, though, I wonder what Anthony Trollope would have thought of me? I know what I think of *him* (turning out as many as five books a year!), but I daresay his twig-bending days were vastly different from mine. Anyhow, I take as a personal affront these comments from his auto-biography: "I have known authors whose lives have always been troublesome and painful because their tasks have never been done in time. They have ever been as boys struggling to learn their lessons as they entered the school gates. . . . I have not once, through all my literary career, felt myself even in danger of being late with my task. I have known no anxiety as to copy. The needed pages far ahead—very far ahead—have always been in the drawer beside me."

Dear, *dear* Anthony Trollope! A task given to *him* meant a task accomplished, with no ifs or buts, whereas a task given to Lucile . . . but I guess this is where we came in with skin-em-arinkie, dinkie, dye?

One thing, I hope, is clear: there is no evidence . . . none whatsoever . . . that my green years were anything but green. I repeat, *green*. Not flaming red. Nor were they what you might call roaring.

I am, rather belatedly, making a great point of this in order to jack up my rating on the homefront. That is, to convince my children that I was *not* a close friend of Al Capone back in the twenties. My initial mistake, of course, was in not settling the matter sooner. The boy I dated in high school was called "Al" all right, but no one will now believe that I can't remember his last name. And his picture, pasted in my memory book, is definitely on the swarthy side. . . .

But here's what happened. There is nothing quite so depressing as a child's face looking up, holding wonder like a cup, and saying: "Mother, tell us about the olden days."

This is even more depressing when the query follows hot on the heels of, say, a session of homework involving the Boston Tea Party. Maybe there's no connection but you can't help putting two and two together and sort of wondering. What *do* they mean by "olden," anyway? To me, the word "olden" ties right in with King Arthur and the Round Table.

In self-defense, then, I have . . . over the years . . . been careful to identify myself with the Roaring Twenties. Actually, I only came in on the tail-end of the roar but it simplified matters (and even added a little Scott Fitzgerald glamor) to thus pinpoint myself in history. Surely, it was preferable to be identified with Clara Bow rather than Guinevere? Surely.

Then along came that TV documentary film on the twenties, with the late Fred Allen supplying a running commentary, and I was stuck with my story. I, along with my open-mouthed children, stared in fascination at the whole frantic scene: Al Capone and his machine guns; Texas Guinan yelling "Hi, Sucker" in smoky night clubs; flaming youth gurgling bootleg gin in rumble seats; chemise-clad cuties, with their rolled stockings, flailing their arms and legs in the Charleston.

"WELL," said my daughter, as I snapped off the TV. "So *that's* your period, Mother." (Suddenly, she struck me as looking *very* austere in her St. Mary's uniform.) "And who did you say that boy was you dated? Al . . . *who*?"

There was small point in protesting that I, myself, had never handled a machine gun or spent my evenings rapping on speakeasy doors. No point, either, in saying that I hadn't *even* been the life of the party: dancing on top of pianos. (I, if you will recall, sat down *at* the piano.) The evidence was all against me, even to my old ukelele still up in the attic.

So you can see for yourself why I sometimes wake up at night and worry about that anthropologist. My memory book just doesn't *begin* to reveal the true "Lu" Hardman, class of '27, with her ways so very real, her matchless appeal!

Gardens are Good for People

"Gardens are good for people," writes Dr. Frank E. Molner, M.D., in his syndicated health column. "Gardens keep you out in the fresh air. Working in the garden is a good way to give you some mild exercise, such as bending over. Gardens even keep you from smoking too much, sitting too much, drinking too much, nibbling too much. Oh, there are lots of good things about gardens, and they look nice."

This sort of masterful synthesis, as with some of the finer passages from Hemingway, always leaves me pretty depressed. That is, Hemingway always leaves me with the feeling: "What is there *left* to say about bull fighting? He's *already* said it, and so well. What could *I* possibly add?" And into the wastebasket go all my notes on bull fighting . . .

Likewise, after Dr. Molner, what is there *left* to say about gardens?

In his clear limpid prose (and if there's anything I like,

it's a medical man who doesn't talk over my head), the doctor seems to have captured, and in just a few sensitive strokes, the essential charm of gardens for all time, from Eden on down. They (gardens) keep you away from the house . . . sitting, nibbling, smoking, drinking . . . and they also "look nice."

Really, I'm sure that nature lovers everywhere will agree that it even makes Gerard Manley Hopkins sound pretty clumsy. Of course, Hopkins *tried* . . . with his "There lives the dearest freshness deep down things," etc. . . . but it just can't stand up in comparison, can it?

Yet much as I admire Molner's style, I have to ask myself one question: this is vivid writing, yes, but is it *honest* writing? I mean, coming from an M.D.

For instance, what is behind that picturesque phrase "mild exercise, such as bending over"? Does he mean bending over to pick a snapdragon, which is my idea of mild exercise, or does he mean bending over a spade, digging a thirty-foot trench to plant a privet hedge? In any event, I'm reasonably sure that the doctor has his waiting room lined with gardeners, all with varying degrees of spinal injuries, from May to October. ("Doc, I was just bending over when suddenly . . . snap! Tell me, Doc. Will I ever walk upright again?")

Too, I'll bet that the good doctor has pulled many a zealous gardener from death's door after a too-enthusiastic spraying of DDT. Also, what about all the minor ailments he has surely treated, such as Black Widow bites, sun stroke, torn ligaments, infected blisters, hay fever, and possibly even a few cases of lockjaw from stepping on rusty rakes?

Gardens are good for people, sure, but *which* people? The laity or the medical profession? Compared to the perils of gardening, the sitting-nibbling-smoking-drinking regime, safe in one's own living room, could be downright healthy.

Again, what about the psychiatric injuries? What about that woman in Rhode Island—recently hauled into court for malicious trespassing—who climbed over the fence, in the dead of night, and dumped bags of salt on her neighbor's petunias? Presumably, or at least as I reconstruct the crime, her own petunias . . . despite the utmost loving care . . . hadn't been doing too well. Her neighbor's had. Then came the day when the neighbor leaned over the fence, just once too often, and said: "I simply can't understand it. *Anyone* can grow petunias. Why, every filling station in the United States has petunias. They even grow around the gas pumps."

There then followed the bags of salt: another sad, but perfectly understandable, re-enactment of the Biblical sowing of the tares. Human nature just doesn't improve very much with the years, does it?

This leads us, directly, to the problem of over-fixation. Many a man, avoiding the Oedipus complex, has later succumbed to the Dahlia complex. Only the other week I read of a divorce trial where the injured wife, bitterly complaining that she hadn't had a vacation in sixteen years, pointed the accusing finger at her husband's prize dahlias. (With a circumference, as I recall, of 11½ inches. How measurements can, and do, lead a man astray!) Her husband's vacation, reported the wife, always fell due in August and he refused to budge from home just as his dahlias came into their glory. He just kept saying, "Why, Maude dear, what has the seashore got compared to all *this*?"

Don't know how the case came out but, incidentally, have you ever noticed how murder—especially in the British mystery thrillers—is so often traced to a little old can of arsenic in the potting shed? Flowers, for some reason or other, always seem to demand such lethal nourishment that the opportunities for doing away with unloved parties are practically unlimited. And since no one ever suspects the gardener himself ("people who love flowers just *have* to be good people") this is often rough going on the other characters: the butler, the village idiot, the neurotic aunt from Sussex who just dropped in for the week-end, etc. Me, though, I always suspect the flower fancier right off the bat. There are even moments when I don't trust Nero Wolfe himself, always puttering around with those black orchids of his.

Nor can you tell me that the innocent-sounding African Violet Clubs, whose meetings I follow with great interest in our local society column, necessarily breed good will toward all men. For one thing, these indoor gardeners aren't getting any fresh air or anything. Rather, they can smoke and nibble and drink *while* raising violets and I suppose, by spring, they're in pretty poor shape. Anyhow, judging from what I read in the paper, the nervous tension must run pretty high at times. For instance, I recently read a very heated and controversial piece that carried the big black headline: KING OF HOUSE PLANTS FALLS. (Actually, the headline was only a *little* smaller than the one about Sputnik II.) And, as I read it, I couldn't help thinking how it might undermine the whole social structure of the violet clubs:

"For many years African violets have been the top favorite among house plants but now I sense the trend is moving away from them and on toward other less demanding members of the Gesneria family. At the risk of alienating readers by the dozens, and making enemies by the hundreds, please let me say that I couldn't be more happy about the whole thing. In my opinion, African violets have always been grossly overrated and have been the cause of more frustration, among indoor gardeners, than any other single plant. In all sincerity I feel that Episcias, Columneas Streptocarpus and other gesneriads can be much more rewarding and with much less effort."

This strikes me as a pretty hot-headed dissertation (perhaps written by an expelled club member?) and I only hope that I, in quoting it, haven't offended anyone. Honestly, I only mention it because it bears out my thesis about gardeners in general: a touchy, high-strung, temperamental breed, living right in our midst, who had best be handled with velvet gloves.

Yet let us not, despite the sinister dangers and hidden passions connected with gardening, completely lose our heads. Rather, let us consider . . . calmly, and without panic . . . Man's innate hunger for beauty and Man's ultimate end. After all, flowers *do* look nice and, since we all have to go sometime, what better way to die than with a trowel in one's hand? When you look at it that way, it isn't half so frightening.

However, I *would* like to let you in on my own successful, and really quite sane, method of gardening. The secret of success, I feel, lies not so much in the condition of your soil but in the position of your house. I refer not so much to a North or South exposure as to . . . well, not to get too technical, I just mean the *position*. Which way it's facing.

For instance, it just so happens that my own back yard doesn't fall within my line of vision. Thus causing little or no pain. But by a benevolent stroke of fate, one of those benevolent strokes that so rarely come my way, both my kitchen and breakfast-room windows command a sweeping view of my neighbor's flower garden: throbbing with color from early spring to late fall. The view is also quite excellent, I might add, from our second-floor bathroom.

She's really a splendid worker, my neighbor, and her well-planned garden (and my view) has improved at a *most* satisfactory clip over the years. In particular, I applaud her recent decision to rip out the candytuft, circling the bird bath, in favor of the moss roses. Never did care for that candytuft. Too, I'm pleased that she finally transplanted those big white flowers (peonies?) a little closer to the driveway where I can see them better. Now, if she'd only thin out those clumps of pink phlox . . . which I feel were a mistake to begin with . . . and plant a few more of the yellow dwarf-rose bushes . . . but there, there, I don't mean to carp. On the whole, I'm terribly satisfied with her work.

It does seem rather a pity, though, that my neighbor . . . when day is done . . . is obliged to sit on *my* back steps if she wants to enjoy her own handiwork. A pity, too, that all she can see from *her* windows—thanks to the Whitcomb and Keller Real Estate Company—is my back yard in all its pristine purity (i.e., untouched by human hands). It's a sorry exchange of views, yes, but I still say she has no real grievance. I mean, I understand that a plain green color scheme (and that's my yard, plain and green) is very soothing on the nervous system. Use it all the time in hospitals.

I suppose, though, that it all boils down to a question of Viewpoints? And viewpoints, as we know from the United Nations, aren't always so united. That is, I sometimes wonder if my neighbor—as she stares broodingly out her kitchen window—is quite as philosophical as I about the status quo. (My philosophy, straight from Aristotle: "Well, that's the way the cookie crumbles, the ball bounces, the ginger snaps, the mop flops.") Does she sometimes mutter to herself,

"Well, it wouldn't kill old Hasley to at least plant a geranium or *something* for me to look at"?

Still, you can't say that I don't . . . in a hundred thoughtful ways . . . try to make things up to her. Why, I'm even thinking of donating some tulip bulbs (much as Queen Wilhelmina once cemented good relations with Washington) for along her back fence. Frankly, I'm very partial to tulips and have never been able to understand why she doesn't like them. Claims they're a nuisance to dig up every year, but what kind of an excuse is *that*?

I also occasionally wave to my neighbor . . . a bright cheery wave of encouragement . . . as she trudges along our shared driveway, lugging several miles of garden hose. Or as she straightens up from her weeding, arching her back for a moment's respite after all that stooping and squatting.

Certainly, it's hard work—all that spading, seeding, sprinkling, transplanting, weeding, hoeing, raking, spraying, mulching—but there's nothing more rewarding, I always say, than a beautiful back yard. And as I gaze dreamily out my kitchen window, thoroughly enjoying the view as I wash the dishes, I sincerely hope that my neighbor keeps up the good work.

Buried Treasure

The handwriting is perfectly legible. The directions are
crystal clear. And with any luck at all, such as hitting a nice
rainy spell, I imagine that the ingredients could be very
easily assembled.

Hence, there's no reason on earth why I can't . . . when
and if the mood should ever strike . . . brew myself a batch
of what my mother calls, and so rightly, her "artificial"
maple syrup. The recipe reads, in her neat Palmer School
penmanship: "Soak 10 corncobs (clean) in 5 quarts of rainwater for 1 hour. Then bring slowly to a boil and boil ½
hour. Strain, add 6 lbs. light brown sugar and boil as thick
as strikes your fancy. The white cobs, to my notion, make
the nicest looking syrup."

I have no questions. The supermarket has never yet failed
me and I'm sure that down *one* of those aisles, probably
right in plain sight, is a bin of clean white corncobs. Maybe,
for all I know, they even have jugs . . . or cartons? . . . of

rainwater for sale. In any event, the store manager has always been very nice, to date, about ordering items that are currently out of stock.

So, the syrup presents no *real* problem. The only thing that puzzles me is that, across the bottom of the recipe card, Lottie (alias my mother) has written enthusiastically: "Delicious! I have made this *many* times! Roe doesn't care for it."

Surely, I like to think, this is just an innocent *non sequitur?* Just a wifely notation, perhaps with hurt undertones, as to my father's likes and dislikes? I mean, I can't quite believe that my mother would have gone to all that bother . . . brewing up five quarts of sweetened rainwater at regular intervals . . . just to *annoy* a man.

But whatever qualms I may have, in regard to both the purity of Lottie's intentions and the syrup itself, I must say that this particular recipe has one outstanding virtue. *Directions! It comes with directions!* The rest of my legacy (my mother's lifetime collection of choice recipes, passed on to me when she died four years ago) requires dark occult powers of thought-transference that are simply beyond me. I simply . . . but wait a minute. Correction, please.

The other day I *did* find one other documented recipe, squeezed in between Icings and Sauces, that I had overlooked. It tells me how to make whitewash. And, as with the rainwater number, I am perfectly willing to share it with the outside world:

"One-half bushel of quick lime which must be slacked with boiling water. Keep covered during slacking. Strain and add one peck of salt that has been dissolved with hot water. Boil and strain 3 lbs. rice. One-half lb. Spanish whiting and one lb. clean white glue dissolved in warm water. When all is well mixed let stand for a few days to cure."

Here, I *do* have one question. The lime and Spanish whiting and glue, of course, are standard staples in my kitchen but . . . how *much* hot water do I slack with? Lottie doesn't say. She does, however, offer me this general reassurance at the bottom of the recipe: "Painted fruit cellar 5/12/26. Turned out real good. I find the whitewash works best if applied hot."

Also, to be scrupulously fair about this whole thing, I should report that there is actually another recipe, with directions, but it has one minor flaw. No name. I can tell, from the ingredients, that it's at least edible, but what does it *make*? Written on a government card, and mailed from Columbus, Ohio, in 1932, the recipe goes thusly:

"Dear Lottie: I meant to call you Monday morning but Mildred came just as I finished packing and I was in a hurry to get started. I had to go to the dentist but I got fixed up and have worn my bridge ever since. Dora found that recipe you asked about last Sunday and so here it is. [There then follows this nameless creation.] How is Bessie? Are her legs still bothering her? Love, Myrtle. P. S. I don't know *why*

you must whip 1 tbls. of water with the cream but that's
what Dora said."

Well, so much for the practical and workable—if not
mouth-watering—part of my inheritance. We now come to
the bulk of my estate: the delicious and time-tested recipes
that I can almost taste (so sharp and vivid are both my
memory and my yearning) but that, as far as I'm concerned,
might as well be down in Davy Jones's locker.

I *know* there's buried treasure, snug and safe in that little
wooden recipe box, but I can't . . . simply can't . . . break
down my mother's secret code signals. Nor does hope lie
along the visual-recall method, even though my mother—
as Queen Bee in the Hasley kitchen—spent the last eleven
years of her life with us.

Unfortunately, although it seemed like a diplomatic move
at the time, I always gave the Queen Bee a wide berth in
the kitchen; never hung around the mixing bowl with eager
cries of "Ooh! May I *please* watch you just this once, Mommie?" Besides, I knew all along . . . see? . . . about those
neat and nicely-written recipes, stashed behind the electric
mixer. What Old Smarty Pants didn't know, of course, was
that they'd be as easy to decipher as the Dead Sea Scrolls.

It isn't so much the walnuts and hickory nuts that bother
me ("Add butter, size of") as the maddening word "usual."
That is, Lottie's idea of a perfectly adequate set of instruc-

tions goes like this: "Make usual batter a little thinner than usual." Or, "The secret of this cake is in having the oven hotter than usual." Or, "Add ingredients in usual order."

Occasionally, she will abandon the over-worked "usual" in favor of the flattering phrase: "Use your own judgment." (Use your own judgment as to seasoning, length of baking time, consistency of sauce, etc.) Another favorite phrase of hers is the cryptic expression: "If handy." (If handy, you might add some beaten egg whites. If handy, toss in some raisins.)

These two phrases, combined, leave me with something like this: "Use your own judgment as to seasoning but take it easy on the nutmeg. If handy, I like to add a little left-over pickle juice. Adds snap."

This I can well believe. My mother had a passion for utilizing left-over pickle juice, if handy, and one of her favorite tricks . . . that is, until my husband put his foot down . . . was "rinsing out" the catsup bottle. Loath to abandon the last hard-to-shake-down teaspoonful, she would add sundry liquids . . . pickle juice being the most palatable . . . and give it a good swish. "Just rinsing out the bottle," she would say, all innocence, to the first unsuspecting victim to choke on it.

But aside from the souped-up catsup, which was never an outstanding success in our household, my mother's sense of taste was unerring. Come to think of it, it *had* to be, considering her native repugnance for definite measurements. And maybe she took a lofty pride in just being guided by her taste buds? Anyhow, I admit that I take a certain miserable satisfaction in recalling her annual conflict with the Church of Rome: possibly the only organization in the world that *could* thwart her cooking-by-taste routine.

That is, she always had to prepare the sausage dressing for the Christmas turkey on the night before: Christmas Eve, a day of fast and abstinence. "Humph," she'd mutter darkly, stumping around the kitchen in high dudgeon, "I'd just like to see the *Pope* make this dressing without being able to taste it." Still, as if guided by radar, she and the dressing (with its yard-long list of ingredients but nary a single measurement) always came through with flying colors. Once again, and until the next holy Yuletide season rolled around, peace reigned between my mother and the Vatican.

Another recipe destined to perish from this earth, and whose passing I mourn, is called Lottie's Lick'em. Although my professor-husband always gagged at the title, this was actually a delicious relish that graced our table for years. But, quoth the Raven, nevermore. The recipe goes along in fairly intelligent fashion until I hit this: "Add some ground allspice, tied in a bag, to the above ingredients. Grind and boil all together."

Asks the Raven: "Yes, but what happens to the *bag*?"

I realize, of course, that this might not distress a really professional cook, one who cooks with bags everyday, but I . . . the unworthy (*non sum dignus*) daughter . . . am geared to directions that leave little or nothing to the imagination. (Like: "Do not thaw. Bake in 350° oven for 25 minutes. After 15 minutes, remove the tinfoil.") And while I have acquired certain culinary skills . . . such as clawing my way through cellophane and tinfoil and pliofilm in double-quick time . . . I am easily intimidated by directions that *snap* at me.

For instance, I just might attempt Lottie's Hot Milk Cake, always one of my favorites, if only the directions didn't scare me so badly: "You have only 60 seconds to dump everything together and fold. *Do not dawdle!* This is no time for puttering!" I know I shouldn't take this so personally but I seem to hear, across the years: "Lucile! For heaven's sake, put down that cigarette! A white sauce has to be stirred *continuously.*"

If nothing else, though, there's a certain nostalgic aura about these recipes that I just don't find on the back of package mixes. It's practically like riffling through the family album and coming across half-forgotten relatives and neighbors, now immortalized forever as "Aunt Mable's Yum-Yum Pickles" or "Marguerite's Devil Food" or "Mrs. Dabrowiak's Delicious Chewy Cookies." (Unlike the publishing world, there are no copyrights to worry over. The original owners wouldn't have a leg to stand on, in court, versus Aunt Mable, Marguerite, or Mrs. Dabrowiak.) But you see my point? Somehow, I just *don't* have the same folksy feeling toward Duncan Hines or Ann Page or Betty Crocker. Besides,

Duncan and Ann and Betty don't have personal little comments, at the bottom of their recipes, for me to mull over.

Marguerite's Devil Food, for instance, carries this triumphant notation by Lottie: "*I* varied this by mixing hot coffee with the buttermilk. Turned out *much* better than M's." Even more triumphant is the comment under Lottie's Burnt Sugar Cake: "Took this to the Bengalese missionary meeting. Everyone asked for recipe. They hardly touched Sadie's sponge cake at *all.*"

All this is my idea of a good evening's reading, but my husband, for some reason or other, is growing more and more fretful. You might even say panicky. I mean, he still persists in thinking that I could, if I *really* put my heart into it, manage at least to duplicate Lottie's potato salad. "After all, you do have the basic recipe," he says, at regular three-month intervals, "and that's the main thing, isn't it? So couldn't you just *try* and remember . . . ?"

So I try again. I try as hard as any patient, stretched out on the psychiatric couch, to reach back . . . and back . . . to the Missing Chord.

First, I see about twelve even-sized potatoes, in their jackets, cooling on a rack. Next, I see them diced up very small, along with some unidentified greenery, in a large shallow dripping pan. The next thing I recall, and it's a pretty wide gap, is *unveiling* the finished product on the beach at Lake Michigan; smugly listening to the squeals of my friends: "O Boy! Mrs. Hardman's potato salad!"

Since those carefree and happy days, my packaged potato chips have elicited virtually no squeals at all. Certainly, not from my husband. But what can I *do*? My legacy, which is entitled "Lottie's Special Potato Salad" and sub-titled "Just the way Louis likes it," reads in its entirety:

"Prepare the usual ingredients the night before and chill. At last minute, pour special sour cream dressing (the 3 egg one I got from Mrs. Vargo) over mixture and toss lightly with fork. Do not *mangle*! If handy, add a little dill pickle juice." And then, across the bottom, she has casually added: "This dressing is tricky to make. Curdles easily."

And I, if this were only a two-way communiqué, would write back: "Lottie, tricky isn't the word for it. The word is *impossible*."

Still, as I try to tell my husband, my legacy is most certainly not a total loss. We *do* have a lot of beautiful gastronomic memories, which is more than some families have, and we *do* have some interesting reading material to pass on to our children. I mean, why should recipes . . . for heaven's sake . . . be necessarily linked with eating? It doesn't follow. Anyhow, as Bacon said, reading maketh a full man.

One (1) Nasturtium

No matter what the psychologists say, *I* like to think that I have an open mind. Biased and retarded, maybe, but open. (That is, subject to sudden change overnight.) Yet have you ever noticed how the psychologists, when this switcheroo takes place in a *female* mind, just shrug it off as a "woman's privilege"? Don't give us any credit at all for being so . . . well, so reversible? Instead, they just shrug their shoulders, throw up their hands, and mutter things like "Wouldn't you know?" and "Oh, brother!" and other unscientific terms. Even husbands sometimes pick up this deplorable lingo.

Me, though, I like to use words like "open" . . . "flexible" . . . "receptive" . . . "delightfully unpredictable" . . . "not hidebound."

For instance, I may say things like "I wouldn't be caught *dead* in a knee-length sack dress" or "You couldn't *hire* me to eat lamb kidneys" or "I'd never entertain Molotov in *my* living room." I even speak in italics—so strongly do I feel—

and yet, so delightfully flexible is my mind, I just *might* break down someday on all three scores. (Actually, now I think it over, those aren't really very good examples. Maybe you'd better just forget them?) Perhaps a better and more concrete example of a laudable change of heart would be . . . well, you might take that essay I once wrote about gardening. I didn't exactly say that gardening was for the birds but I did imply that the birds could have it if they wanted.

Certainly there was nothing in the chemistry of the soil that called out to *my* chemistry. *Au contraire,* I had long since concluded that I was the original Kiss o' Death Rosie as far as all plant life was concerned: that I either had an absolutely lethal touch or (more logical) the plants just naturally preferred death, and as speedily as possible, to living with me. With one lone exception (an unattractive but virtually indestructible plant called Mother-in-Law's Tongue), all forms of green life . . . once they were carried over my threshold . . . immediately exhibited this neurotic will-to-die compulsion.

Now I didn't mention all this in my original essay (too touchy a point with me) but you can see for yourself why I built up my defenses. That is, you can take just so much rejection and no more and, in this particular instance, I soon began to feel hostile toward the plants themselves. If they didn't *want* to live, I certainly wasn't going to sit up nights coddling the little beggars: pleading that life *could* be beautiful, *was* worth the candle, and that nihilism was a highly decadent philosophy. Somehow, I just don't have the patience of Bishop Sheen.

And then one fine day, Mother's Day of 1957 to be exact, I received three potted geraniums, all gloriously swathed in crinkly tinfoil, for the sun porch. When they didn't, like their predecessors, wither and die within the week, I began to do a double-take. What was wrong? Was it possible that these geraniums really *liked* me?

It was a very giddy sensation, believe me. Quite went to my head. Maybe, I thought in my giddiness, I might even extend my green thumb prowess to the back yard? Sort of surprise my know-it-all neighbor next door? Have her look out her kitchen window one fine morning and be literally blinded by the riot of color I had wrought?

It also occurred to me that it might be very pleasant to saunter out in one's own garden . . . a straw basket over one's arm, clipping shears in hand . . . and gather a dew-drenched bouquet. (Never once had my neighbor urged me to pick her flowers, no matter how lavish my praise.) I was possibly also swayed by my fondness for British writers, all of whom . . . according to their personal journals . . . puttered happily around in (or at?) the "bottoms" of their gardens. (Have never looked up this expression but I presume it means the rear end of the lot? In my case, this would mean where the incinerator and alley meet.) Anyhow, I was always coming across casual little observations like "A kingfisher haunts the stream that runs through the bottom of my garden" and, although bird-watching always left me cold, it certainly conjured up a pretty picture. Personally, I don't know *anyone* with a stream running through their back yard. All that runs through mine is a stream of neighborhood kids playing touch football.

But let us return, however reluctantly, to the American scene and stay there.

My approach to gardening can best be described as "furtive." To me, there seemed something faintly disreputable about a grown woman planting her first nasturtium seed at an age when she *should* be cross-breeding gardenias or something. It wasn't at all the same thing as the middle-aged women (the newspaper accounts of which left me steeped in admiration) who suddenly took up skin-diving, ran for Congress, or returned to high school to graduate with their grandchildren. *That* was inspiring. *This* was ridiculous. It was sort of like a woman . . . after twenty years of housekeeping . . . suddenly deciding to learn how to make French Toast.

Hence, I contented myself with a few discreet queries from my most intimate friends. What flowers were absolutely fool-proof? Could you really trust those colored packages of seeds at the supermarket? How did you know when the last frost was over? Did the seeds need any special nourishment to get going?

A seed was a seed, said my friends. All it needed, under God's providence, was sun and rain. "And be sure to keep stripping the flower beds," they added. "Especially the nasturtiums. They multiply faster that way."

They were much more explicit, though, about the *etiquette* of gardening. The sporting thing to do, they said, was to start from scratch; not buy any fledgling plants at the city market. However, it was quite acceptable . . . indeed, I gathered it was something like exchanging autographs in a school memory book . . . to receive shoots and bulbs from your friends and relatives. *Then* you had something to talk about when you conducted a guided tour around your yard. Like: "See that snowball bush over in the corner? Aunt Etta gave me a shoot off her bush . . . oh, it must've been ten years ago when I visited her in Sandusky . . . and just look at it now. It was touch and go, though, that first year. Real sickly. Then, it just seemed to catch hold. . . ."

This, then, seemed the essence of a *real* garden . . . memories, tradition, crucial illnesses, loving care . . . and it occurred to me that I, with my little 25¢ packages of seed, had a long row ahead of me. I mean, how did you get people to crash through with their donations? Should I send out gilt-edged invitations: "Mrs. Hasley, who has now taken up gardening, will receive donations from 3 to 6 next Sunday"? Anyhow, I'd better get the ground all churned up and ready. . . .

I didn't mind the initial spadework at all. It was even quite pleasant, what with the two big shade trees protecting me from the sun and with the cunning little gophers to

keep me entertained. They, the gophers, were really *so* cute
the way they'd squat back on their haunches, arms folded,
and look me coolly in the eye. At first, I couldn't decide
whether it was a look of cool admiration (after all, I *was*
breaking virgin ground) or a look of cool contempt, but now
I think . . . yes, contempt.

Anyhow, those first weeks of anticipation were really
among the happiest I'd known. I even, now that I'd rejoined
the human race and become a gardener, started to read
The Home Garden column (somewhat similar in tenor to
Ann Landers) in the Chicago *Tribune* every morning.

Goodness, I thought comfortably, the problems *other*
people were having! Here was a man in Gary whose elm
trees were afflicted with phloem necrosis. Here was a man
in Evansville whose corn, just as the ears ripened tenderly,
was stripped by the gophers. (Solution: Take tin cans,
remove both ends, and place the cylinders over the ears like
a suit of armor. A pretty little scene, I should think, providing you first removed the Campbell soup labels: the
shining knights riding off to the great crusades.)

And while none of these problems were mine (indeed, I
had none), I *could* join the spirited and even passionate
controversy over our proposed national flower. Yeah, how
dare that Senator So-and-So propose the lowly corn tassel!
It was unthinkable, with or without tin cans. And yet the
rose, everyone's favorite by a sweeping majority, had already

been selected by England. Did we dare, especially after the Suez Canal flare-up, create an international crisis by. . . . ?

My head swimming from the various problems and decisions that faced us gardeners, I would then saunter out . . . master of the estate . . . to inspect the progress. Amazing! Man, that green fuzz was really coming along! (That is, it wasn't quite like the slogan said: "Plant Mandeville seeds and jump aside"—but it was *coming.*) It was even coming up in the children's abandoned sandbox where I, trustful to a degree, had patted down some aster seeds. (Asters, said the printed directions, did well in sandy soil.)

Finally, after morning and night feedings, I felt that it (the green fuzz) was ready for transplanting. Carefully, and with all the skill of a laboratory technician, I replanted the fragile blobs of green life according to directions. Such as: "Petunias must be planted far apart, for they are a leafy plant that spreads rapidly."

Oh? Mine grew tall, skinny, spindly. To date, and it is now late August as I write this report, there have been exactly eleven blossoms. Pretty blossoms, yes, but eleven. My score in the nasturtium bed, and I will swear this before a notary public, is one (1) blossom. The zinnias along the fence have done somewhat better (and so they should, if they have any pride at all, being Indiana's state flower), but it would be more effective, I think, if they bloomed at the same time. Not just one by one. As for the asters in the

sandbox . . . well, they're an autumn flower, you know, and
so I really can't tell as yet. But shouldn't they, by now, be
more than two inches high?

"I think you've done real well," says my neighbor. "Everything looks real *tidy*. But if you want to raise flowers, you'll
have to chop down those shade trees and kill the gophers."

And I, like Barbara Frietchie, say NEVER. There shall be
no mayhem in *my* garden. Indeed, I would no more pick
one of my poor blossoms (the question of gathering a bouquet does not arise) than I would behead one of my own
children. Rather, to tell the truth, I feel quite tender toward
my retarded garden. Can *it* help it that, two inches below
the surface, there spreads a vast labyrinth of twisted tree
roots, studded with young boulders, where dozens of cool-
eyed gophers run up and down the corridors, munching
nasturtium roots? You'd be retarded too.

Besides, I tell myself, masses of flowers can be so confus-
ing, even rather vulgar, as versus a shy and delicate blossom
standing out all by itself. Now you take the Japanese, and
they're a really artistic race, with their floral arrangements:
the loving appreciation of *a* lotus blossom, *a* twisted root, *a*
single branch of pear blossoms. That is, the true nature lover
. . . like the poet with his "O, flower in the crannied wall" . . .
can read more meaning into a single and isolated miracle.
And as I gaze at my one embattled nasturtium, the meaning
I read is this: "Yankee, go home. Quit annoying the natives.
The gophers got here first."

But I tried. You can't say I didn't try. Indeed, you might put me in the same category as the two-year-old boy (described in one of G. B. Stern's books) who was awarded a prize, by his elders, because "he ran valiantly and *in the right direction.*" Which is lots better, of course, than running ever so swiftly in the wrong direction . . .

And even though I ended up with a very tidy, and highly Oriental, garden that perhaps wouldn't appeal to everyone, I must say that it's very conducive to holy meditation. That is, this business of *counting* one's flowers . . . much as saying one's rosary . . . can be very salutary for one's soul. It's very difficult for Pride to get the upper hand in a garden with one (1) nasturtium.

The Case of the Retarded Mrs. Hasley

It is quite possible that I may someday . . . I repeat, someday . . . write an absolutely stunning tribute to Our Lady: a tribute so stunning and so profound that all Christendom will tremble from the impact.

It is also quite possible that this prediction (exclusively my own) may strike a few of my readers as being a wee bit balmy. They may even be so unkind as to wonder if I've taken up opium. . . .

Actually, though, my reasoning is quite simple. You know that old adage about still water running deep? Well, have I ever been *still!* Indeed, one might think—as far as Our Lady is concerned—that I, like Zachary, had been stricken dumb in the temple. In other words, I base my prediction of an absolutely stunning tribute (so all right, then, a half-way decent one!) not on my past performances at the typewriter but, rather, on my quite appalling silence. For instance, I don't believe I ever once—during my entire two-year stint as weekly columnist for the *Ave Maria*—mentioned the name of Mary. A dubious distinction if I ever saw one. And when various editors, over the years, requested essays based on my "personal devotion to Mary," I have had but one stock answer: "The greatest favor I can do for Mary is to keep quiet!"

Now I might, in order to save face, offer up the facile explanation that I—like one of the early Desert Fathers— had taken the vow of silence in reparation for all the things that *shouldn't* have been written about Mary. It makes a plausible case. The honest truth of the matter, though, is that my "devotion" to Mary—at least compared to the lyrical outpourings of other writers—has been a very retarded and slow-budding affair.

This is not to say, of course, that I've been a *complete* clod. I can respond to much of the poetry (e.g., Gerard Manley Hopkins' *The Virgin Mary Compared to the Air We Breathe*) and *all* of the straight theology but . . . somewhere along the line . . . I seem to have become Mary-shy.

Why? I really don't know. All I can say is that possibly it's because so many good people, in trying to push *their* particular brand of Marian devotion, manage clumsily to kill it for others. Too, I admit that I . . . as an ex-Presbyterian . . . haven't been too edified by the born Catholics who seem to have a lop-sided devotion: the ones, for instance, who pack the church for a novena to Our Sorrowful Mother but rarely turn up at the communion rail.

Yet such is my truly reverent desire for a solid and genuine devotion to Mary that I, well aware of my "psychological injuries," refuse to hasten the thing artificially. I feel it must come slowly and naturally, to be any good, and I therefore beg my readers (my horrified readers?) *not* to deluge me with devotional pamphlets or miraculous medals. Frankly, I'm loaded! I prefer, if you don't mind, to leave it in Our Lady's hands: let *her* handle this case (The Case of the Retarded Mrs. Hasley) in her own good time.

In the meanwhile, I can—honestly, naturally, and easily—thank Our Lady for having sent, most directly, two of *her* own special friends into my life. I haven't the faintest doubt that she did arrange this—for she didn't cover her tracks too well!—and this, perhaps more than anything else, convinces me that I'm not a lost cause.

First of all, then, there was Caryll Houselander—whose classic *The Reed of God* (easily the strongest and most beautiful book I've ever read about Mary) so swept me off my feet that I, in the white heat of the moment, dashed off my first fan letter. I knew she lived in England—and that her publishers might, or might not, be in the mood to forward a letter with insufficient postage—but it didn't too much matter. I *had* to get it off my chest; *had* to tell her how, after all the drivel I'd read over the years, her book had made Our Lady sound appealing. More important, it made theological sense.

Imagine, then, my startled joy when I received an eight-page letter from 810 Nell Gwynn House that was signed "Love, Caryll." I couldn't have been *more* overcome had it been signed "Love, Queen Elizabeth." True, the handwriting was utterly miserable and the spelling and punctuation were even more so, but the letter, in itself, was something for the archives. I'm quite convinced that Caryll couldn't write a lifeless sentence . . . or even hit the wrong word . . . if she tried. More important, she was . . . quite simply . . . stretching out her hand to me, over the Atlantic, and saying: "It's clear that you and I were meant to be special friends."

Now this is more than passing strange—especially when you consider that Caryll is known as a "mystical" writer, whereas I am anything *but*—and yet our long friendship (stemming, mind you, from her Mary book!) was what you might call a "natural." Even more strange was her insistence that my essays (dealing with American family life and thoroughly saturated with American slang) were—and I quote, red-faced—a "source of strength and joy" to *her*.

Of course, one need only read her book, *A Rocking Horse Catholic*—published shortly after her quite recent death—to realize that hers was a very strange and lonely life. It explains, perhaps, her flaming awareness of the Mystical Body ("We all share the Passion in a thousand secret ways") and her equally flaming conviction that suffering should not be wasted. One of her last letters to me . . . saying how willingly and even *gladly* she accepted her approaching death from cancer . . . made you, on reading it, want to make the sign of the cross.

Surely, she had more empathy toward the misfits and derelicts and sinners of this world than anyone I ever knew. To quote from one of her letters: "But the older I grow the more unwilling and afraid am I to preach. That's why I prefer to write fiction. It's more like a big gesture of sympathy . . . like taking hold of another sinner's hand and pressing it lovingly as we, not looking at each other's faces, walk along together." And if she herself was "neurotic" from childhood (and what a devastating childhood it was!) well, then, one can only wish that all the neurotics of this world could contribute a fraction as much as she to the leavening of the loaf.

Caryll abhorred organizations . . . believed firmly in the personal contact . . . and knew, in her heart, that that was the only way for her to operate. Again, I quote: "You ask how I deal with my correspondence. Well, it simply defeats me, Lucile. I get letters from all over the world, mostly from poor little people in real trouble of soul or body. Sheer fan mail I seldom answer for I want to save myself for those who really do need help. I have reduced myself to four hours' sleep at night and still it is never done. Well, I daresay this shows no prudence . . . but if Prudence is the so-called Queen of Virtues, then I prefer to consort with the charwoman of virtues!"

Perhaps, for all I know, it was this same fine disregard for prudence that led to her unleashing *me* on an unsuspecting public. Anyhow, it was Caryll who . . . having dinner one night in London with Frank Sheed . . . urged him to "follow up" this friend of hers who lived in Indiana. From this contact, then, resulted the publication of my first book, *Reproachfully Yours,* and it was only proper and fitting, of course, that Caryll should write the foreword. I say "proper and fitting" although I assure you that you may never again —between the covers of a single book—find two such strange bedfellows.

Now one might think that my other special friend . . . crossing my path through the courtesy of You-Know-Who . . . was an equally odd selection: a semi-cloistered nun whose every breath and gesture is dedicated to Our Lady of the Cenacle! Anyhow, this nun one day wrote me a note introducing herself. Like myself, she was not only a convert but an ex-coed from the University of Wisconsin and it appeared (judging from an essay I'd written) that we had—all unknowingly—been students at the same time *and* entered the Church during our senior years.

These vital statistics so charmed me (especially the thought of a once atheistic coed who was now called *Mother D.*) that I couldn't resist her invitation to visit the Cenacle Convent in Chicago someday. I took pains to warn her, of course, that I wouldn't be coming for a *retreat* (indeed, that I was allergic to retreats) and that I was also

somewhat gun-shy when it came to nuns. Priests were fine
. . . you could really *talk* to priests . . . but nuns (or at least
the violets-hidden-under-a-mossy-stone type) were something else again. But, I said, I'd like to drop in sometime just
to say "hello" . . . perhaps between trains on my next lecture
trip. . . .

Yes. Well, my "drop in" wasn't exactly like *The Man Who
Came to Dinner*—I didn't trip and break my leg on the front
steps—but I *did* virtually collapse in the convent parlor. My
first memorable words were: "Hello. It's *me*. Can I please
go to bed?"

I'll never know exactly what hit me (although I suspect
it was the cumulative strain of my sick mother, who was to
die six months later) but I know I was put to bed in double
fast time. And as this nun whipped around the room . . .
lowering the shade, fetching aspirin, shoving in a hot water
bottle . . . I couldn't help saying: "Behold the handmaid of
the Lord!" I said it teasingly, of course, but the conviction
grew on me, that week-end, that I had said a mouthful.

Later I became a star boarder at the Cenacle, it being
a perfect oasis on a traveling junket, and I *even* made my
first retreat: St. Ignatius' Exercises and all! (That "and all"
means the awe-inspiring phenomenon of a group of women
maintaining silence.) Moreover, I am here to tell the world
that a Cenacle nun (whose apostolate, after all, is that of
spiritually reviving her weary and battered sisters out in the
world) is a very valuable find, indeed. I think, too, that

there are times when only a woman can understand another woman. (No need, surely, to explain the female nervous system. Or those mornings when you get up feeling like eight miles of bad road.)

But to return to Mother D. It would make very dull reading if I were simply to list her various virtues, in alphabetical order, and give no inkling of the delightful person behind that veil and wimple. Yet something tells me that the Cenacle might take a dim view of a vivid and personalized "Toast of the Town" tribute and hence I must, most regretfully, content myself with a few questions.

Have you ever known a nun who had a mind like a shining steel bear trap? Or, to put it more gently, a mind that seemed the living counterpart of *Theology and Sanity*? And ever known a nun who combined this strong type of masculine mind with the equally strong, but highly gentle and compassionate, virtues that make the word "Mother" spring easily to the lips?

Now this may sound extremely silly (and I advise all theologians to plug their ears at this point) but I one day said to her, out of the clear blue sky, that it would be mighty helpful if I could think of Our Lady (with her fancy titles of Tower of Ivory, Star of the Sea, etcetera) as being as real and strong a person as she. Would she mind, I asked, acting as a substitute *pro tem.* for the Mother of God? Then I waited for her anguished scream of protest.

No scream. She understood exactly what I meant and,

without batting an eye, said she'd be very happy to pinch-hit. I guess, maybe, that she figured anything was fair in love and war?

So there you have my two special "Mary" friends . . . one in Heaven and one in Chicago . . . and I'm so deeply grateful that it almost gives me pause. I mean, there are moments when I can almost persuade myself that I do . . . in my own quaint fashion . . . have a "devotion" after all.

Let Nothing You Dismay

(A Christmas fantasy, to replace Scrooge's
annual appearance on TV)

The eight Gratchet children . . . from Tiny Tom, aged
three, to Ben Junior, aged twenty-two . . . trooped wearily
into the house at 10 P.M. They were tired, true, but had put
in a good evening's work: canvassing the entire South Side,
since six o'clock, for the Halloween trick-or-treat handouts.
Ben Junior carried a loaded gunny sack . . . the others, bushel
baskets . . . and even Tiny Tom (being only three) had a
stout shopping bag strapped onto his back.

As the children dumped their haul on the living room floor
. . . apples, popcorn balls, candy, cookies, bubble gum, and
a little loose change . . . Mrs. Gratchet clapped her hands
with pleasure. (She was one of those wise mothers who like
to applaud her children's smallest efforts.) "I declare, children," she now said, "I think this is the best year ever! Why,

there are almost enough apples to see us clean through the winter. I may even be able to can several quarts of apple-sauce. Isn't it splendid, Father?"

Ben Senior removed his pipe and said gruffly: "You're good children, all of you. And now, Mother, why don't you fix some hot chocolate for everyone? The children must be hungry."

"Not me," piped up Tiny Tom. "I've eaten six Hershey bars, three Tootsie Rolls, two Turkish Delights and . . . and one old lady even made me a milk shake."

Mrs. Gratchet ruffled his hair indulgently and joined in the general laughter. "*Someone's* going to have a good tum-my-ache tonight and maybe even a nightmare," she declared merrily. "But who cares, eh, children? Halloween comes but once a year!"

Later, as they sipped their hot chocolate, twenty-two-year-old Ben Junior said thoughtfully: "Mom, do you think I'm getting too old for trick-or-treating? One man laughed at me. Asked if I didn't belong on the night shift at Bendix."

"Nonsense!" said Mrs. Gratchet, indignantly. "Children are only young once, I always say. And now off to bed, all of you! I'll pick up, and sort out, all the goodies on the floor and . . . oops, Tiny Tom! You've stepped on a cookie. Don't grind it into the carpet, sweet."

Tiny Tom's blue eyes filled with tears and Mrs. Gratchet, dropping to her knees, cradled him to her. "Mother's sorry," she crooned. "Mother didn't mean to speak so sharply to

her baby. Look, sweetie, Mother will step on another cookie
. . . see? Mother doesn't *really* mind."

But Tiny Tom, over-tired, remained tearful. Indeed, he
was now bawling his head off. Mrs. Gratchet stepped on still
another cookie, grinding it into the carpet, but even this did
not check the poor little fellow's screams. On a sudden inspir-
ation, Mrs. Gratchet clapped her hands and cried: "Children!
Children! I have the loveliest surprise for you! Guess what!
Guess what I heard over the loudspeaker at the supermarket
today! *Christmas carols!*"

Mr. Gratchet glanced up sharply. "I say!" he exclaimed
with real pleasure. "That *is* good news, dear. If there's anything I like, it's a long long build-up to Christmas. Can't start
too soon to suit me! Why, I think I'll even drop into the
supermarket tomorrow and personally commend the store
manager. If enough customers show their appreciation, next
year he might start the caroling right after Labor Day."

Mrs. Gratchet nodded happily. "It's certainly something
to shoot for, isn't it? And from now on, the newspapers will
be so loaded with Christmas advertising that we can hardly
find the editorials. And soon the street decorations will be
going up . . . and all the TV singers will start reviving
Rudolph The Red-Nosed Reindeer. . . ."

The eight Gratchet children, transfixed with joy, now
found their voices. "Mommie, Mommie!" they shouted. "Can
we start making paper chains and gilding nuts and stringing
popcorn and making out our Christmas lists?"

Mrs. Gratchet threw up her hands in mock dismay. "Hadn't I better clean up the Halloween stuff first? And don't forget that there's still Thanksgiving. But tomorrow, I promise, we'll start marking off the days on the kitchen calendar. And now, off to bed, the lot of you! No, Tiny Tom, you *can't* stay up to watch *Nightbeat,* but I tell you what. Would you like this molasses popcorn ball to take to bed with you? After all, Halloween comes but once a year!"

The days sped by merrily for, to tell the truth, all the days were merry at the Gratchets'. They were not blessed with worldly wealth . . . indeed, they were heavily in debt . . . but they had a nice sense of values. Mr. Gratchet, who ran an elevator, did not mind spending over his head in order to buy happiness for his children. Nor did Mrs. Gratchet mind knocking herself out providing a lavish table, with all the festive touches.

Soon it was Thanksgiving. Mrs. Gratchet, her ankles badly swollen from being on her feet since five o'clock that morning, had baked three apple pies (apples from Halloween), four mince, five pumpkin, and one lemon chiffon. Not all the children, you see, liked the same sort of pie. Indeed, Tiny Tom didn't like *any* kind of pie. For him, Mrs. Gratchet had made a three-layer burnt-sugar cake with a large turkey, outlined in pink, on the frosting.

As Mr. Gratchet carved alternately from a turkey, capon, rabbit, and baked ham (for the children had varied tastes

here, too), Mrs. Gratchet . . . at the other end of the heavily
laden twelve-foot table . . . tossed an enormous salad. None
of the children, of course, would touch a salad but she always
kept hoping. Ben Junior, at twenty-two, no longer screamed
when she placed a teaspoonful of shredded lettuce on his
plate . . . just let it lie there, untouched . . . and Mrs. Gratchet
thought this a very good sign, indeed.

As soon as the plates were loaded and grace had been said
(Mr. Gratchet inserting a word of thanks for *all* holidays,
past, present, and future), the children could contain themselves no longer.

"*Now* can we start making Christmas things, Mommie?"
they cried. "You said . . . you *promised* . . . we could start
right after Thanksgiving."

Mrs. Gratchet, her eyes misting happily, smiled at her
brood. "I've got the paint, paste, paper, glue, and scissors
all ready for you, lambs. From now until Christmas, Daddy
and I will turn the living room over to you . . . we'll call it
Santa's Workshop, shall we? . . . and Daddy and I will retire
to the sun porch. I think we'll be warm enough if we plug
in that little electric heater and bundle up good, don't you,
Father?"

Mr. Gratchet smiled his assent. "The house belongs to the
children," he said. "I only pay the monthly installments. But
would it be all right if I moved my easy chair onto the
porch? That wicker furniture always jabs in my back."

"Is that all right with you, children?" asked Mrs. Gratchet.

"Remember, Christmas is the time to be kind to people. Besides, if we take out Daddy's chair, it'll leave that much more room for your pasting and painting."

Ben Junior, gnawing a huge drumstick, spoke up as their rightful leader. "I'll make a deal with you, Mom," he said. "If Daddy keeps his chair, couldn't *I* please string up the electric lights on the tree this year? I'll be twenty-three in February and I *know* I could do it. I'll bet I could even pick out a better tree than Dad, too."

Mrs. Gratchet glanced uneasily at her husband. "But that's always been Daddy's fun, son. You *know* how he likes to pick out a tree that's too tall and lop-sided and then saw off the branches and wire and nail them on again. It took him almost four hours, reconstructing last year's tree, and a fine job it was. As for the lights . . . well, he always *so* enjoys hunting for faulty bulbs when the whole string blows out."

Ben Junior had the grace to hang his head. "Sorry, Dad," he said gruffly. "I guess I was being pretty selfish."

Mr. Gratchet cleared his throat with some difficulty. In times of deep emotion, he could never think of the right words. "You're a good lad, son" was all he could now manage.

This crisis safely past, Mrs. Gratchet suddenly clapped her hands to her head. "Heavenly days!" she ejaculated. "I plumb forgot to serve the mashed potatoes and gravy and dressing . . . and now you're all ready for the pie."

One and all, they laughed until the tears came to their eyes. "I guess the joke's on me," declared Mrs. Gratchet, wiping her eyes with one corner of her apron. "Oh, well, that's part of the fun of holidays, isn't it? And now for dessert! Tiny Tom, Mother has made a big cake just for *you*. You . . . you what? You don't want any? You want an Eskimo Pie instead?"

Mr. Gratchet was already on his feet. "It's all right, Mother," he reassured his wife. "I'll run right down to the corner drug store and get one. After all, Thanksgiving comes but once a year!"

The days sped merrily by. Three weeks before Christmas, the last hand-painted card had been sent out; the last wreath hung; the last package wrapped.

"I declare, Ben," said Mrs. Gratchet, making a rueful little face at her husband. "I almost wish I had it to do all over again."

Arm in arm, they surveyed the small mountain of packaged gifts at the East end of their bedroom. Even their gift for the newsboy was elaborately gift-wrapped, with real silver bells and mistletoe nestling in a swirling red satin rosette. "It's a beautiful sight," agreed Mr. Gratchet, "but what time did you get to bed last night? It must have been after four. But no matter! Tell me, dear, have you remembered to enclose the sales slips in all the children's packages?"

Mrs. Gratchet, her eyes slightly bloodshot, looked reproachful. "What a question, Ben! That's half the fun of

Christmas . . . returning gifts the next day. Would I be likely to forget the slips? Besides, you know very well that the children like to check the prices themselves and see that no one comes out ahead. They're *such* funny little dears."

"And speaking of funny little dears," said Mr. Gratchet, "what about Sandra and Eloise? Have they picked out the Christmas formals they wanted or are we just giving them a blank check?"

"Neither," said Mrs. Gratchet, with a fond little smile for her nineteen-year-old twins. "They decided that the formals were just part of their regular upkeep and shouldn't count as Christmas presents. Of course they're right, dear, when you stop and think about it. So they asked for two new Hi-Fi consoles instead."

"Good deal!" ejaculated Mr. Gratchet. "This year's models, I understand, have many improvements over the '57's. And I'll hustle right down to the finance company tomorrow and see if I can swing a larger loan. Would you mind, dear, if I had to put up those cemetery lots we own as collateral?"

"What a funny boy you are, Ben," said Mrs. Gratchet playfully. "You know I always put first things first, especially at Christmas time. But oh, how I wish I had it to do over again . . . I mean, all the shopping, and getting caught in revolving doors, and getting smashed in the crowds. Somehow, there's such a crazy magic excitement about it all! But then," she added, her face brightening, "there'll *still* be a lot of last-minute hip-hip-hooray, won't there? Filling the eight stockings . . . cleaning the house . . . having the neighbors in for egg-nog. . . ."

"And don't forget the big buffet supper on Christmas night for all your relatives!" Mr. Gratchet glowed at the thought of all the second and third cousins on his wife's side whom he hadn't seen since last Christmas. "I'll bet our liquor bill will even exceed last year's," he chuckled. "They all voted against having hot spiced rum again, you remember. In fact, your brother Bill offered to send out several cases of his special bonded Scotch and let me pay him later. Said I could have up to New Year's to reimburse him."

"That's my Bill," murmured Mrs. Gratchet. "Even as a little tyke, he was always so thoughtful and generous. And Cousin Ethel has offered to bring along a pint of her watermelon preserves. . . ."

Mr. Gratchet bent over and kissed his wife on the brow. "I know, it sort of gets you, doesn't it?" he said softly. "There's just something about Christmas that brings out the best in people. I just have no patience at *all* with the cranks who . . . well, did you read that editorial in last night's *Tribune*? All that tripe about the crass commercialism of the Christmas season . . . and people running themselves ragged keeping up with the Jones's . . . and the false and sloppy sentimentality? It really burns me up."

"I know," said Mrs. Gratchet, nodding wisely. "*Some* people just don't know how to have fun. Why, do you know what Tiny Tom was telling me only yesterday? You know those new people who moved in down the block, the McDugals? Well, Tiny Tom says they're having a *green* tree with a little manger underneath! Really! What sort of a tree is *that* for children to enjoy? Green, indeed. And Tiny Tom also said that the McDugal children only get *two* presents apiece, outside of their stockings, and have to keep what they get. Even worse, those poor children have to go to Mass on Christmas morning before they open their gifts. Ben, do you think I should DO something? I mean, notify the Child Welfare department?"

Mr. Gratchet tamped his pipe thoughtfully. "Odd," he observed. "I once met McDugal and he seemed a decent enough chap. But no, I think we must try and give them the benefit of the doubt. They're probably poor people for one thing, trying to live within their income, and haven't caught on to installment buying. And many of these people, just over from the old country, still cling to the customs of their ancestors. That is, they still regard Christmas and Easter as religious feast days in some of the more backward countries. I read all about it in one of the *National Geographics.* Real quaint customs: Advent wreaths, mangers, Midnight Masses, having their priests bless food and things."

"I declare," said Mrs. Gratchet, shaking her head in wonderment. "I'm as broadminded as the next person but it somehow seems so unfair to the children. So sort of pathetic. I tell you what, Ben! I think I'll pack the McDugals a Christmas basket of goodies . . . and maybe send along Tiny Tom's electric robot from last Christmas that he never liked . . . and see if I can't cheer them up somehow. What do you say, Ben?"

"I say you're the Spirit of Christmas in person," declared Mr. Gratchet fondly. "In fact, I think it calls for a carol! Come on, dear . . . we've only got three more weeks to sing them . . . and so what shall it be? Oh, here's a good one to harmonize on! 'God rest you, merry gentlemen, let nothing you dismay. . . .' "

Whatever Lola Wants, Lola Gets

I wonder, does anyone know of a nice quiet sanitarium—preferably with reasonable rates and a good therapy class in basket weaving—where I can take the cure? I don't insist, of course, on the basket weaving (I daresay a class in pottery would do just as nicely) but the "reasonable rates" is quite important. I may be in for quite a stretch.

My doctor also stipulates, by the way, that the sanitarium have no library facilities; no incoming magazines or newspapers; and that all Book-of-the-Month Club circulars be carefully winnowed from one's mail. Also, he wants assurance that no well-meaning relatives—who might conceivably try to cheer up the patients with some Positive Thinking pamphlets—be allowed on the premises. Also, no TV. There's to be no slipping out of bed and feverishly twisting the dials to Norman Vincent Peale's *What's Your Trouble?* program. After all, as my doctor points out, my trouble *is* Dr. Peale.

Yes . . . well, I suppose we all have our own particular breaking point, don't we? Still, it does seem rather strange. I mean, I managed to survive all our *other* national epidemics of recent years: the two-week egg diet, McCarthyism, Liberace, Davy Crockett. . . .

Anyhow, it seems that I'm to get what they call the "cold turkey" cure and I know . . . especially after watching a dope addict on *The Line-Up* the other evening . . . that it's not going to be very pretty. Already I can see myself, tossing in torment on my rumpled cot, and begging a beady-eyed matron: "Please! Please, matron, you just don't know what it's like! Can't you slip me just a little shot in the arm to tide me over? Maybe . . . maybe just *one* of Peale's *Confident Living* columns?"

No, it won't be very pretty: a grown woman like me, whimpering for my narcotic build-up: my daily supply of carefully selected quotes from scripture. (Incidentally, this is a service that Catholicism doesn't offer me, *i.e.,* this careful screening of quotes to make me feel good. Why, *my* pastor —insensitive creature that he is—is just as likely as not to come out with some of the most distressing things! Things like: "I bring not peace but a sword" or "What doth it profit a man if he gain the whole world . . . ?") But as I started to say—and you must forgive my rambling digressions, it goes with my condition—the really pitiful thing is that the Positive Thinking "lift" wears off quite rapidly. Say, in about fifteen minutes. Then, time for a new shot! Time to get my "spiritual batteries recharged"!

For a few intoxicating moments, though, I am able to whisper to myself: "And why not? Can't I do all things in Christ who strengtheneth me? Why *can't* I become a top executive with U. S. Steel?"

You haven't heard the worst, though. It's true that Dr. Peale is the high priest, as it were, of Positive Thinking (alias "the cult of reassurance"; alias "the selfish religion with the easy answers"; alias "the God-and-me-can-do-anything narcotic fad"), but it's a wide-open field, with no holds barred. There are plenty of *other* P. T. boys (now jumping on the gravy boat) to tempt me from the straight and narrow. And when I say tempt, I mean *tempt*. Really, you have no idea how utterly fascinating it can be, once you throw off the deadly shackles of doctrine and balance and common sense.

Hence, I can see myself, during this forthcoming cold turkey treatment, becoming very crafty and cunning as the fever mounts. For instance, I have long been expecting the P. T. boys to come out with a book called *How To Never Have To Die* (it seemed the next logical step in the "How To" series) and I think the glorious day may be just around the corner.

At any rate I recently spotted an ad for a book called *Get a Victory Over Death* ("This can be accomplished by KNOWING HOW, and should be the aim of all men") and

I'm just afraid that my growing desire for this . . . in the still watches of the night . . . might lead me to attempted blackmail. That is, blackmailing my friends (and I have several good prospects lined up) into smuggling it past the sanitarium gates: perhaps baked in a cake or buried in a pot of geraniums. So while I have the temporary strength of character—that is, with my doctor twisting my arm—I'm sending out this general appeal: "Friends, don't DO it!"

Of course, the worst wrench of all . . . indeed, I get a lump in my throat just thinking about it . . . is my doctor's dictum that I must throw away my scrapbook. It's a veritable treasure trove, my scrapbook: chock-full of helpful Positive Thinking suggestions that might come in very handy someday. For instance, what if I should someday want to lift a four-hundred-pound barbell? Well, listen: "In order to lift a four-hundred-pound barbell over your head, it is first necessary to think it up there. Muscle helps . . . but without the thought the muscle is superfluous."

Muscle helps. I quite like that careless admission, don't you? But if barbells leave you cold, *here's* a priceless tip that will surely appeal to one and all: how to pick up a little ready cash without, presumably, having to work too hard. I quote:

"Meditate and ask God if there is any reason why you should not have the thing you desire. Dismiss your desire for a few days and if it is right for you to have it, the desire will become more intense. This removes doubt and uncertainty and inspires determination and action. . . . If you desire money, visualize the amount and feel it in your pocket."

Standing, maybe, in front of Tiffany's with a rock in your hand?

Actually, I'm sure this isn't what the author of *How To Turn Your Ability into Cash*[1] had in mind, but when there are no ethical qualifications . . . well, what other response can you expect from an evil-minded reader like me? Anyhow, let us proceed to one of my favorite quotes of all time: a perfectly law-abiding set of instructions for the person afflicted, as am I, with stage fright. As you totter across the stage, pea green with terror, you have only to remember:

"Cast your eyes easily over the audience for a few seconds, smile and look pleased. . . . Breathe deeply and fully many times. Stretch and press down on the diaphragm. Repeat the Lord's Prayer and feel its presence. Thank God for the opportunity, the occasion and the people."

Frankly, I think it sounds practically fool-proof. The only reason I never got around to trying it out, on my lecture trips, was because I couldn't quite figure out what the *audience* would be doing all the while I was smiling and breathing and praying and stretching and pressing. Mightn't they get restless?

And then, here's a little eye-opener that I picked up somewhere or other: "The Bible teaches that longer prayer time means a longer lifetime. Why not pray longer and live

[1] Earl Prevette; New York, Prentice-Hall, 1953.

longer? Why not increase the length of your life by increasing the length of your prayers?"

Do you know, I never before had realized why the Little Flower had died in her early twenties? Why, the wretched girl just obviously wasn't praying enough. Of course, the biographies all insist she died of tuberculosis but . . . a likely story, a likely story.

And here's a little credo of "I believe's" that I picked up . . . thought it might be useful on a Wednesday afternoon (doctor's day off) in case an emergency arose: "I believe that God who can make a star can stop a toothache" . . . "I believe that Jesus, who can move mountains of stone, can move the little gallstones from a person's body." . . .

But enough. There's no point in tormenting myself. My little scrapbook, over which I have spent so many happy hours, is now to be liquidated.

The doctor tells me that if I co-operate, and sweat it out for myself, I just may . . . in perhaps six weeks or so . . . be given a little light reading as a test run. Say, the telephone directory—and then possibly work up to *Bre'r Rabbit*. However, he insists that I am never again to touch as heady fare as the "How To" series (*How To Become Rich, Beautiful, Happy, and Dynamic in Just Ten Days . . . How To Enjoy the Beatific Vision Right Here on Earth . . . How To Never Get the Idea that Anyone Else Is Possibly Smarter Than You Are*) because I just haven't got the constitution to touch the stuff.

In particular, he warns me that he just won't be responsible for me if I ever again try reading—within a twenty-four-hour time span—two such books as *The Secret of the Saints* and *How To Turn Your Ability into Cash.* He says the delicate membrane of the human stomach just can't tolerate such a deadly mixture.

I've also, incidentally, had some other close shaves with disaster. Without first testing the depth, I plunged into Peale's *The Power of Positive Thinking* as if I were plunging into the *Summa Theologica* and I . . . well, sir, I darn near broke my neck in the shallow water. As I later discovered, there was barely enough water—theologically speaking—in which to do the Dead Man's Float.

Just the same, I have to admit that I just *couldn't* seem to grasp Peale's message. I didn't know whether it was my native stupidity . . . or the fact that I didn't have the pure heart of a child . . . or whether I'd become tone-deaf from listening to too many TV commercials. Anyhow, the horrid truth is that I seemed to react to Dr. Peale in much the same way as John Crosby did to Liberace.

Mr. Crosby, you will recall, is the fearless TV columnist and critic who enraged American womanhood from coast to coast by writing: "Somehow, everything that Liberace plays comes out sounding like *Lady of Spain.*" Yes . . . well, everything that Dr. Peale wrote came out sounding to me like the song novelty *Whatever Lola Wants.* ("Whatever Lola wants, Lola gets" . . . a real Positive Thinker, that Lola . . . right down to her punch line of "I'm irresistible, you fool.")

Actually, it sounded quite delightful (especially when I transposed it to "Whatever Lucile wants, Lucile gets"), but how did one go about it? Honestly, I couldn't seem to figure out even the simplest directions. For instance, Dr. Peale told me that I should start the day by repeating "I believe" three times and—providing one can count up to three—what could be simpler? But me. No, I had to have the sort of snoopy mind that asks: "I believe . . . *what?*" Since Dr. Peale didn't tell me (he has apparently taken the Pledge to avoid all doctrine as if it were poison ivy) I was right back where I started. That is, I had no choice but to muddle along with my usual Morning Offering.

Distressing? Frustrating? I'll say. But there's a certain cold comfort, you know, in *finally* discovering what ails you.

Now this may come as a nasty jolt to you . . . I'm sure it was to me . . . but the doctor has finally decided that I have a 100% Peale-Proof mind. This was not a hasty decision on his part, I might add, but the result of extensive testing. For instance, he would first read a quote from some Catholic spiritual writer and then a quote from Dr. Peale (without, naturally, identifying them) and then closely observe my reactions. It was a terribly interesting experiment—in fact, you may well watch for it on a future *Medic* program—and I'd like to give you a tiny preview.

One of the sample quotes, for example, was from Friedrich von Hugel: "Some people are so fond of ideas. A new idea is a kind of magic to them! I don't care about ideas. I want facts. God is not an idea. He is a fact. . . . I don't much like all this Coué business ('Every day in every way I am getting better and better'), all this dwelling on ourselves. Leave ourselves—let in God."[2]

They tell me that my reaction was highly positive. I not only seemed to grasp the meaning but my eyes brightened; I nodded; I smiled; I even said: "Wow! That's telling them."

Then they tried a Peale quote: something about an insurance salesman who had tripled his quota by sticking an "Ask and ye shall receive" card on his windshield. Believe it or not, they tell me that my eyes grew glazed and vacant and that, to the best of their knowledge, the words simply *did not penetrate*. 100% Peale-Proof!

The doctor says that I can learn to live with this disability; indeed, lead a fairly normal life; but that I must naturally be very careful. Especially when it comes to P. T. books dealing with mental hygiene. He says that even a normal reader can go quietly off his rocker trying to sift out the *good* mental health rules from all the secularistic hogwash.

"After all," he says sternly, "what gave you this horrible case of E. I. I. if it wasn't a book on how to *avoid* E. I. I.?"

Now as everyone knows, E. I. I. stands for "emotionally induced illness": a perfectly valid medical concept of many of our ailments. For instance, you can actually develop a pain in your neck from a passing emotional disturbance (e.g., watching your husband splash catsup on even his dessert) and this Dr. John Schindler had *more* than proved his point. Just the title of his book, as a matter of fact, was

[2] *Letters to a Niece;* Chicago, Regnery.

enough to make my old neuralgia, that hadn't acted up in years, go on the rampage: *How To Live 365 Days of the Year: A Tested Method for Living Without Sickness, Fear, Fatigue, or Nervous Strain.*[3]

Or high Christian purpose. He should definitely have added that to his title, but maybe it just wouldn't fit on the book jacket? After all, he already had quite a mouthful: all those golden promises to restore man to his original Garden of Eden status.

Well, Dr. Schindler was obviously cutting his own throat . . . offering a Tested Method that would neatly wipe out the entire medical profession . . . but that was his concern. Not mine. *My* first unselfish thought was: "Oh, dear, what a beastly shame! If *only* the Early Christian martyrs and all the saints throughout the ages could have profited from this book! If *only* they had had the proper KNOW-HOW for avoiding all the suffering (not to mention the fatigue and nervous strain) that goes hand in hand with Christian heroism. Poor stupid St. Paul, poor little St. Lucy, poor. . . .

Dare I say poor *Christ* in the Garden of Gethsemani? Strangely enough, it would seem that He wasn't praying in the right fashion at all.

Let me quote, painfully and meticulously, from Dr. Schindler's instructions: "Many people find prayer a ready way for starting a pleasant stream of emotion. But it is important to get into prayer the same attitude of calmness and cheerfulness. For instance, it would not do to pray like

[3] New York, Prentice-Hall, 1954.

this: 'Oh, Lord, I feel miserable, and the situation I am in is terrible. Won't you help me, God?' The supplication should run more like this: 'Thou hast created a wonderful wonderful world for our enjoyment. Give us the courage, equanimity, etcetera, to enjoy this wonderful life.' . . ."

Offhand, this didn't strike me as a very good all-purpose prayer. Couldn't you maybe get away with a short anguished yip of "MY GOD!" if you were falling off a precipice? Or if you were perched on a housetop sailing down the flooded Mississippi? Or, to go to the other extreme, what if you were stranded high and dry in aridity? Wasn't there supposed to be a certain grace in gritting out prayers (of the "Here I am, Lord . . . as cold and blank as a mackerel . . . but *here I am anyway*" variety) even if it *didn't* start a pleasant stream of emotion? And what about the Catholic "offering up of suffering" angle? Personally, I had always liked Father Considine's consoling little thought: "A lonely heart offering its loneliness to God, a stricken soul simply exhibiting its wounds . . . this is to pray indeed. Our need is our sufficient argument."

Suddenly, the full impact of this lop-sided "wonderful wonderful world" business hit me smack between the eyes. Good grief! The Pope was going to have to call another Council of Trent and throw out the Psalms (they sang out *both* joy and suffering), revamp the Mass, eliminate the Stations of the Cross (not cheerful enough), erase Lent from the liturgical cycle, and . . . most assuredly . . . kick out the confessional. Might not shame and sorrow, even with relief just around the corner, give us a passing twinge in the colon?

Final conclusion: Brother, the Church sure *doesn't* have the necessary KNOW-HOW.

At this point, the appalled reader may ask why I was reading Dr. Schindler in the first place. A nice question. Answer: it happened to be a Catholic Book Club selection.

"But," says the Appalled Reader (dropping *that* like a hot potato), "aren't you being awfully nasty, making fun of that nice Dr. Peale who is only trying to spread a little sunshine?"

Frankly, I think that anyone who defines religion as a "workable and useful mechanism for preventing energy leaks" is spreading *more* than sunshine. Besides, the sort of sunshine I like stems from the positive thinking (small p, small t) of the saints. You might even call it the spiritual gaiety of those who put first things first: "Seek ye first the Kingdom of Heaven . . ."

You might even call Lourdes the mecca of positive thinking at its best: the faith of the lame and the blind and the halt that they *may* be cured, but without the "Whatever Lola wants, Lola gets" insistence that their will comes first. And what the uncured pilgrims take away with them is often more precious than their restored vision or straightened legs: an uplifted heart, full of love for a God who answers prayer in His own fashion. Not at the dictates of Lola.

The Pencilling Mama

Theoretically, a writer's personal life should be of small concern to the public but, for my money, it's often of more passionate interest to me than his actual writing.

I don't mean, of course, that I go in for any key-hole snooping on authors . . . or that I recruit victims for Mike Wallace at so much a head . . . or that I even check on their Easter Duty or income tax returns. I just have a healthy interest in what their friends and relatives think of them, that's all. And you can surely use the word "healthy" when the biographical data are right in plain sight at the Public Library?

Anyhow, I find that the essays of Alice Meynell are somewhat too exquisite for my Mid-western palate but that her daughter's book about her famous mama (*Alice Meynell, A Memoir*, by Viola Meynell[1]) is pretty fascinating stuff. Oh, it's not exactly as highly charged as the material in

[1] New York, Scribner's, 1929.

Confidential . . . I grant you that, right off . . . but the fascination is there, all right. At the same time, it sends horrid little shivers down my backbone: just toying with the grisly possibility that one of my children, potential Benedict Arnolds that they are, might someday be tempted to write up *their* mama.

This is not to say, of course, that there is any striking resemblance between Mrs. Hasley and Mrs. Meynell. She, I would have you know, was so idolized as a literary figure in England that Max Beerbohm once commented: "In a few years Mrs. Meynell will have become a sort of substitute for the English Sabbath." And as for her personal friends . . . well, haul out the literary *Who's Who:* Chesterton, Belloc, Francis Thompson, Coventry Patmore, George Meredith, and so on.

If there still remains any lingering doubt as to our basic disparities, let me say that Mr. Meredith, in reporting an evening of conversation with her, murmured in ill-controlled rapture: "We waltzed together on celestial heights." Another friend, in recounting her impression of Mrs. Meynell, wrote: "The conviction presses in on me that . . . I met a being whom my sceptical mind must reluctantly name a saint."

Now maybe *my* reluctant and sceptical friends are saying things like this, behind my back, but are just safeguarding my humility? Maybe they even, in feverish communiqués amongst themselves, are putting it down in black and white for posterity? Like: "Last Thursday I spent the most heavenly evening with the Hasleys! At first, Mrs. Hasley seemed a little cross (I think she wanted to watch *Playhouse 90*) but, after her husband snapped off the TV, she quit sulking and made the best of it. Really, the conviction presses in on me that I must, reluctantly, name her a saint! And when the conversation, which lagged at first, finally got around to her new dining room wallpaper . . . well, I tell *you,* we really waltzed together on celestial heights."

As I say, this sort of thing may be going on behind my back. But wouldn't you think, honestly, that I'd pick up a stray rumor . . . here and there . . . about all these worshippers from afar? Wouldn't it leak out somehow? Actually, I can only recall *one* friend coming right straight out, in her unbridled enthusiasm, and telling me what she thought of me. She was really quite articulate even though, being Russian-born, she has a little trouble with her consonants.

"Lucile," she said thoughtfully, "I zink zat you have ze sharp tongue." Pause. "I zink zat it covers ze shyness." And then, after a really deadly pause: "I zink zat ze shyness would be *better.*"

Yes, and then there was that Swedish masseuse that I once went to over on Michigan Avenue. She, too, was thoughtful. "It isn't that you exactly weigh too much," she said thoughtfully. "You just have no *shape.*"

Believe me, ze shyness would have been better for that masseuse, too! Never got another nickel out of·me. But perhaps we'd better, at this point, get back to Mrs. Meynell. It's safer.

Where, you are surely wondering, do the celestial Mrs. Meynell and I finally get together? It's simple. The great bond between us is that she (a) had to run a household on a fairly low budget, and (b) she had to write her essays (so essential to that budget) with her loved ones milling around her elbow. And to give you a rough idea of this milling, let me add that she had *seven* small children: a vital statistic that, however marvelous in itself, wouldn't indicate too much monastery quiet around the premises. So how, one wonders, did she . . . and without cracking up . . . manage to turn out such detached and lovely prose? They didn't even have tranquillizers in her day.

My own personal theory, for whatever it's worth, is that life was easier for pencilling mamas back in the Silent Days: no TV, radio, record players, rock-'n-roll, or nightly telephone marathons. (None of this: "*Mama!* You just make that dumb Viola get off that phone! She's hogged it for forty-five minutes already, talking to that stupid Freddy Ainsworth! Remember, please, there are six *more* kids in this family with important calls to make!")

And while I'm sure there was plenty of noise in the background, as our Mrs. Meynell tried to concentrate, it must have been a more or less *human* sort of noise. *Not* the singing of Elvis. *Not* the pounding of hoofs and the sharp crack of pistol shots as Cisco Kid gallops across the TV screen. *Not* the incredible howl-and-twang of *Great Balls of Fire,* shaking the very rafters, and with Mrs. Meynell trying to yell over it: "Viola! Turn that thing *down*! Mr. Chesterton and Mr. Belloc have just dropped in for a visit!"

I'll bet, too, that whenever she was interrupted by a phone call . . . and a low intimate voice breathed, "Mrs. Meynell?" . . . it really turned out to be someone she knew. Not: "Mrs. Meynell? I'm calling for the Yellow Cross Insurance Company to see whether you and your family are adequately. . . ." Or: "Mrs. Meynell? Congratulations! Your name has been selected from the phone book as a possible prize winner! You may win three free Rhumba lessons at the Gazelle School of the Dance if you can answer this one simple question. What famous Civil War general, whose name started with L, was responsible . . . ?"

Really, the more I think it over, the conviction presses in on me that Mrs. Meynell had an absolute breeze. Don't know why I was feeling sorry for her, only four paragraphs back.

Yet of far greater interest to all of us, I'm sure, is how the seven children (what with *both* their literary parents writing at breakneck pace) made out. Daughter Viola, in her chapter called "The Pencilling Mama," offers these tantalizing tidbits:

"They (our parents) were commonly so absorbed when we were with them that we even temporarily lost our names

and were all called 'Child.' My father would say 'Just post
the letters, child!' without looking up to see which of the
children stood near him."

Hmm, wonder what Ilg and Ames would say to *that*.
Child, indeed! In our household, we either say "Hey" or
"Hey, you!" and maintain the personal touch at all times.
But let us back to Viola.

"We understood our mother's abstracted look when she
had her pencil and writing pad; we understood it less when
there were no implements of work."

As Dr. Menninger would tell you, that's serious business
. . . looking glassy-eyed *without* a pencil in hand . . . but
my daughter Janet is most understanding. Just rolls her
eyes and says, "Mother's in her own little world again."
My son Danny, though, comes right out with: "Hey, Mom,
you need a Bell-Tone hearing aid or somethin'? I've asked
you three times already where you hid my harmonica!" And
now, back to the ranch . . . uh, I mean Viola.

"An evening is remembered by a visitor when my mother
suddenly noticed that some family darning was being done
by one of the girls and for the first time a question presented
itself to her which made her ask in dismay: 'Who *has* darned
your father's socks all these years?' "

Frankly, I happen to know who does the darning around
our house. (*And* the cooking, scrubbing, laundry, etc.) But
maybe . . . who knows . . . something is escaping me? Maybe
I, too, will someday exclaim in dismay: "By the way, who

has been emptying the vacuum sweeper bag all these years? The elves?" (This comes to mind, as a possibility, because the Hoover repair man . . . only last week . . . asked me the same thing. Or practically the same thing.)

Yet fascinating as these little glimpses into the Meynell menage are, I think I most enjoyed the letters that the children, precocious to a degree, wrote their mother. Perhaps my favorite is this severe little number, with its manly attempts at spelling, from daughter Monnie:

"Dear Mother, I hope you will in time give up your absurd thoughts about litreture. It makes my mind get quite feverish when I think of the exhaltation your undergoing. I'm getting quite frightened about calling you 'dear mother' because you will begin to take it quite seriously . . . Now mother take my advice and don't be quite so estatic, you'll get on just as well in the world and much better because you'll be respected. Now just you see, Monnie."

I am happy to report, though, that Mother occasionally came out on top. In the little paper that the children edited themselves (composed *under* the library table while the parents composed on top!) was this bit of high literary praise: "There are few real writers alive now. Mrs. Meynell is certainly one of these few that are in existence. She has produced two books which the world ought to respect and venerate. They are perfect masterpieces."

Now that's the sort of literary criticism I admire: perfectly straightforward, mincing no words, and without any mealy-mouthed qualifications. I like, too, the psychological follow-up: "If you read her work you could tell the sort of woman she was. Hers is a very docile temprement and thoroughly synpethitic. When she is singing a synpethitic song you can tell that she must have some excellent powers in her head."

All in all, I must admit that Mrs. Meynell fared very well at the hands of her children. You can see what I mean, though, when I say that any pencilling mama . . . once her children learn how to read and write . . . might well get the jitters. That is, they *say* that writing isn't hereditary but . . . as with t.b. and Bright's disease . . . you have to watch out for tendencies. And when a child has a special motive for writing . . . you know, eye for an eye, tooth for a tooth? . . . it gets pretty frightening. After all, I wasn't exactly bashful about using *them* for material and so why should I . . . ? Nevertheless, as a placating gesture, I inscribed my first book thusly: "To my children—Susan, Janet, and Danny— in the high hope that they won't sue me for libel when they grow up."

Only, I was thinking in terms of lawsuits that could, however unsavory, be settled with a certain amount of dignity behind closed doors. It just never occurred to me, for Pete's sake, that they might start writing compositions about me for English class! Anyhow, about a month ago, my daughter handed me a returned theme, with the provocative title "My Mother," and asked what I thought of it. She also explained that it was supposed to be a thumb-nail sketch of some character, whom she knew intimately, who had a "conflicting" personality. Rejecting her father as being too "even" in temperament, she had landed . . . and without too much hesitation . . . on You-Know-Who:

MY MOTHER

"Drinks coffee by the gallon . . . won't even *try* to learn how to thread our new sewing machine . . . is very proud of her latest hobby, gardening, although I don't know why . . . isn't always too practical . . . doesn't start getting ready to go some place until the last minute but keeps telling Daddy, 'Don't *heckle* me, I'll get there!' . . . likes good books but watches crumby TV shows by the hour . . . is usually understanding . . . loves crossword puzzles . . . hates anything that crawls, even caterpillars . . . is sometimes rather witty . . . always carries her coffee cup into the living room . . . loves people, travelling, and her family."

Yes, but wherein lies the *conflict*? Doesn't everyone in the United States drink coffee by the gallon and watch crumby TV shows? Just don't get it.

My only clue comes from the teacher's one lone notation on the returned paper. Remember that damning statement about me and the sewing machine? Well, along the margin she has written in red ink: "Any other appliances??"

Apparently she really wants to know, what with those two

question marks, but she doesn't phrase it too clearly. Is she asking, "Do any *other* appliances defeat your mother?" Or is she asking, "Can your mother operate anything at *all*?" Either way, I don't like it. I mean, she seems to be trying to establish my exact degree of idiocy in the mechanical field: an investigation I do not smile upon. So, I hurriedly instructed Janet to assure the teacher that I *had* mastered the electric toaster, alarm clock, and washing machine. That I could, with facility, snap on the TV, all light switches throughout the house, and the car ignition. That I had even been known to use the new Long Distance dialing system.

These may be minor points, true, but when my daughter doesn't even *mention* my literary efforts (hence, my sensitive reluctance to point out that I can also manipulate a typewriter!), I have to salvage what I can.

Frankly, though, I don't like this stress on mechanical skills one little bit! Has *everyone* become so Science conscious . . . what with Russia getting a head start with her little old Sputniks . . . that the gentle art of essay writing just doesn't count any more? Or, in order to have a non-conflicting personality, am I supposed to write essays *and* thread bobbins? Maybe even whip up a few home-made rockets in the kitchen?

I just don't know. All I know is that no one pushed Mrs. Meynell into a corner like that. I also know, with a sinking heart, that my mechanical deficiency ties in with a one-line description that Danny once wrote for school: "When I ask

my mother questions about Diesel engines, she doesn't
answer very fast." Yes, but why couldn't he . . . like those
charming Meynell children . . . have had the decency to add:
"HOWEVER, she has produced two books which the world
ought to respect and venerate. They are perfect masterpieces"?

Shorties

Play it Cool, Sister

I wish some psychiatrist would explain to me, free of charge, just *why* I'm so passionately addicted to questionnaires. Surely, it can't be to bolster up my self-esteem, because I tackle even those questionnaires that I know, full well in advance, are going to leave that esteem pretty mangled.

Such as, for example, that annual "state of the world" quiz put out by *Time* magazine. I generally emerge, head both bloody and bowed, with a score that would embarrass even an eight year old: fluffing all the questions about cabinet members in Uruguay (or even, if you must know, in the United States) and coming in strong on only a few isolated sections. Weighty items such as who won the Academy Award for the year and what famous dressmaker had turned the world of fashion upside down, etcetera.

On the other hand, it isn't likely that I indulge in questionnaires simply because of the salutary effect on my hu-

mility. Opportunities along that line come a dime a dozen.
No, there *must* be some other reason and until some bright
psychiatrist comes up with an answer, free of charge, I can
only offer my own simple and unFreudian theory.

Me, I think I like questionnaires because (a) they make
me laugh so hard and (b) because I like to see if I can
outwit the prankster who dreams them up. That is, I like
to play it cool: try to come up with an answer that I *think*
will boost my score or (if it's very tricky) to assume a
cautious "I'm not talking until I see my lawyer" attitude.
In dire emergencies, of course, there's always the 5th
Amendment to fall back on.

I am not now referring to factual questionnaires such as
in *Time*. I mean the sort that requires neither brains nor
integrity: just a certain amount of agility in side-stepping.

Let us take, for example, a questionnaire that once appeared in a national woman's magazine entitled: "Is Your
Husband Becoming a Bachelor?" Even that title was tricky
and open to question. Me, I think a husband is branded
for life: that not even Reno can help him recapture the fine
careless rapture of bachelorhood.

I suppose, though, that the title meant: "Is Your Husband,
Foolish Boy, *Trying* To Act Like a Bachelor?"

Anyhow, the questions were darbs. They couldn't have
been *more* wildly inappropriate to my state of life as a
faculty wife (thus making me laugh real hard) and they
certainly brought out all my talents in full force as far as

the caginess went. I hereby present, in a home version of *The Confessions of St. Augustine,* my mental gymnastics as I zipped through those questions:

1. Does your husband discuss his business affairs with you as much as he did three years ago? (*Business* affairs? You mean like having him ask me if I think the students in English 5 would prefer *Moby Dick* to *The Scarlet Letter?* Well, yes, I guess he does.)

2. Have you and your husband spent all your vacations together during the past three years? (Watch out now, Hasley. This is clearly designed to trip you up, especially since you've already stated . . . in cold print . . . how you feel about Togetherness. And their spies have probably found out that you *don't* like fishing trips. Better not answer this question until you see how your other scores stack up. This could go heavily against you.)

3. Do you spend at least three evenings alone together every week? (I think this is designed purely for belly laughs. We're "alone" together practically 365 nights of the year— that is, as alone as you can be with your progeny, and their friends, in the living room with you. Not to mention the companionship of Cisco Kid, Zorro, Maverick, Robin Hood, Sid Caesar, etc.)

4. Within the last six months, has your husband brought you a little present, not prompted by a special event? (This will take a little thought. I wonder, can you count the 7¢ *Woman's Day* that he always fetches home from the A & P?

Or the new rubber plug for the upstairs wash bowl that he brought me only last Tuesday? But no, the plug was prompted by a special event: me, threatening to leave home if he *didn't* bring it. Hmm, maybe I'd better let this question slide until I make a more thorough inventory around the house.)

5. Does your husband phone you during the day as often as he did three years ago? (Gee, they're getting me worried. What happened three years ago, anyway? They keep using it as a yardstick and I can't even remember six months back. Oh, well, there's no need to stand on the 5th Amendment here. I'm quite sure my husband calls me as often as he did three years ago. Only, why do they think a professor, living ten minutes away from the campus and home most of the time anyway, *should* burn up the N. D. switchboard?)

6. Do you weigh today about as much as, or less than, you did three years ago? (Now, wait a minute, Mr. Fresh Guy. I'm not saying yes and I'm not saying no until I mull this thing over. I know what you've got in mind, all right, but how do you know *you're* on the right track? What if I was so skinny three years ago that my husband wouldn't be caught dead with me on a public beach? In which unlikely event, wouldn't an increase in weight *help* matters?)

7. Do you spend as much time on beauty care and buy as many clothes and accessories as you did three years ago? (Another pitfall question. I have a hunch I should say "Yes": that I've been running up staggering charge accounts

all over town and that I spend most of my waking hours in Francisco's beauty salon. On the other hand, what *quicker* way to make your husband wish he were a bachelor? Oh, this is a pitfall, all right, all right. It ties right in with that nasty question about extra poundage.)

8. Does your husband spend fewer evenings away from home—working, watching night baseball, bowling, etc.— than he did three years ago? (I seem to have got lost somewhere along the line. Whose husband are they talking about? A bowling ball would terrify *mine*. And the standard crack around our house is that he hasn't seen a movie since *The Birth of a Nation,* starring Lillian Gish. As for working at night . . . yes, that he does: grading themes about ten feet away from me.)

Actually, the only questionnaire that I could possibly take seriously would be one designed exclusively for English professor husbands and with questions like: "Would your husband rather see a Jane Mansfield movie or attend a lecture by T. S. Eliot?"

If Jayne won out over Eliot, *then* I'd begin to worry about my drifting bachelor-playboy spouse.

O Philothea!

I wish I could explain, for my own satisfaction if nothing else, just why the *Introduction to the Devout Life* by St. Francis de Sales is as spiritually beguiling in 1958 as it was back in 1609. By all the laws of survival (if by "survival" we mean our modern standards of writing), it should have died a natural death several centuries ago.

Not even the most avid de Sales fan, and they are legion, can deny that he has his purple patches, his flights into a rhetoric that rings oddly on our twentieth-century ears, and that his constant comparisons with Nature are often downright quaint—not to say, in the light of present natural science, highly inaccurate. ("As pearls, that are conceived and nourished by the wind, or by the noise of thunder, have nothing of the substance of pearls, but merely the external appearance; so the virtues . . .," etcetera.) Moreover, the *Introduction* is studded with all those words and expressions that are considered anathema in present-day spiritual writing: "vouchsafe" . . . "alas" . . . "ah! wretch that I am!"

. . . "reproach your heart with the pusillanimity with which it has hitherto strayed."

Pusillanimity? I don't even know what the word means and I'm not looking it up. If I'm guilty of it, I'd just as soon *not* know. I have enough to handle as it is . . . although, come to think of it, it *might* be interesting to spring "pusillanimity" on one's confessor, mightn't it?

So very fancy, indeed, is the writing that we can't repress a sly grin when St. Francis assures us, in his preface, that the book is "merely a collection of good admonitions which I have delivered in plain and intelligible words without bestowing so much as a thought on the ornaments of language, having business of more consequence to attend to." One thinks (or at least *this* one thinks): "Come, come, dear St. Francis. Surely, you must have spent a *little* time polishing up those fancier passages?"

But to give St. Francis the benefit of the doubt, and I guess we can afford to be generous toward canonized saints, it's quite possible . . . for all I know . . . that he *was* writing to Philothea in his ordinary conversational style. It's well known that he, among the saints, was what you might call a "smoothie": a highly educated, socially adept, well-born gentleman who was perfectly at home in the king's court. I can even imagine him, after a spiritual consultation with some high-born society matron, bidding her adieu with a low and courtly bow from the waist; a last courtly admonition to watch out for pusillanimity. . . .

We might even compare, in a way, the Bishop of Geneva

(alias St. Francis) with our own Bishop Fulton Sheen: a man not likely to trip over his own feet in a drawing room or trip over his own tongue at a banquet table. Just a non-tripper in *all* divisions.

But aside from the flowery literary style of St. Francis (and once you get adjusted, it's really most effective), is not his *Introduction* a very old-fashioned and obsolete version of the lay apostolate as we know it today? Certainly we don't find—nor should we reasonably *expect* to find—any references to Catholic Action, the Encyclicals, the liturgy, or social concepts based on the doctrine of the Mystical Body. Yet in his own day, St. Francis was the pioneer of the lay apostolate—opening up, for the first time, a spiritual way of life for the ordinary layman. As he wrote in his preface: "Almost all that have hitherto treated of devotion have had in view the instruction of persons wholly retired from the world; or have taught a kind of devotion leading to this absolute retirement; whereas my intention is to instruct such as live in towns, in families, or at court, and who, by their condition, are obliged to lead, as to the exterior, a common life."

For this alone—this taking up spiritual cudgels for the neglected layman—one would like to award St. Francis a special citation of honor: something above and beyond his title of patron of the Catholic press. But to get back to our original consideration, *why* is the *Introduction* (with its aura of quaintness and its undeniable incompleteness as a lay apostolate manual) still so perennially dear to the hearts of present-day readers? (On the flyleaf of the Hasley copy is a penciled notation showing that my husband has read it, cover to cover, four times. As for me . . . well, I regard it with a special tenderness. It was the *first* spiritual book to really get under my skin. Every time he wrote "O Philothea, wouldst thou not desire . . .", it sounded like "O Lucile, wouldst *thou* not desire. . . .")

So what is the secret of this quaint little classic? Well, for one thing, books by canonized saints are at a premium. The market is not glutted. And it's rather nice . . . don't you think? . . . to get one's instructions straight from the horse's mouth. I mean, it's reasonable to suppose that St. Francis tested out his own material. If he detected any pusillanimity in his heart, he went *after* it . . . and then passed on the recipe to Philothea.

But aside from the fact that the personal spiritual instruction of St. Francis (carrying the Good Housekeeping Seal of Approval!) is still as sound as a hickory nut, I think the *real* secret of the book's appeal is its downright sweetness. Not a cloying sweetness, understand, but a sort of *manly* sweetness. Some of the saints, and we might as well face it, are mighty difficult to stomach; but St. Francis—with his extreme courtesy, gentleness, persuasiveness, sanity, and sympathetic understanding of human frailty—is the perfect guide for what you might call Everyman.

To lapse into the saint's own lingo, he can draw a soul

toward true devotion in much the same way as the sun can make a hard, green little bud burst into bloom. Or to put it in my lingo, I'd say that St. Francis—with his green thumb —is the perfect gardener when it comes to developing and caring for souls, be they orchids or sunflowers.

Why Go to Tibet?

When you live in a pleasant middle-class neighborhood in a pleasant middle-class town in the pleasant middle-class Midwest, it is really rather difficult to imagine extremes in living. That is, the champagne way-of-life versus the skimmed milk way-of-life. (Me, I suppose I fall in the homogenized milk division?) Anyhow, I find both these extremes in my regular reading material . . . namely, *The New Yorker* and the *Catholic Worker* . . . and the contrast, especially at one reading session, is enough to make one's head swirl. It is also, if I may say so, far more fascinating than following Lowell Thomas into Tibet, on his *High Adventure* program, and studying their tribal customs . . . quaint eating habits . . . and economic problems.

Let us, by way of illustration take a peek at the "On and Off The Avenue" section of a pre-Christmas issue of *The New Yorker*. Let the reader, if he will, see how it stacks up with *his* gracious family living:

"Let's begin, then, with what everyone must surely agree is the high point of holiday feasting—that giddy, memorable glass of champagne at the end of Christmas breakfast, drunk while the palate and the day are innocent and while there is still dew on the Christmas tree. Obviously, it takes quite a wine to carry off such a moment, and we like to think that we have discovered in Moet & Chandon's Coronation Cuvee the perfect champagne. . . ."

I wouldn't know about *your* household but the Hasleys wouldn't dream of a Christmas breakfast without that giddy memorable glass of champagne . . . why, it's as traditional as the peanut brittle . . . but the children, fortunately, aren't *too* particular about the brand. In fact, I sometimes have trouble making them finish their drinking . . . they're just that eager to empty their stockings.

But let's get on: "The housekeeper on a budget whose family has acquired a taste for fresh *foie gras* should be interested to hear that unsurpassed goose livers imported by Ellen Grey and priced at $18 a pound can be bought in quantities as small as one ounce."

Indeed, I *am* interested. Danny, in particular, dearly dotes on fresh *foie gras* for his school lunches . . . what small boy doesn't? . . . and yet I admit it does rather throw the budget off center. Toward the end of the month, I've even been known to substitute a peanut butter and jelly sandwich . . . feeling awfully sneaky about it, understand . . . but what can you do? A budget is a budget.

To continue: "What would Christmas be without a new and exciting cheese? Well, we nearly found out, for if Iceland hadn't come through at the last moment with a cheese that had never before left its native land, we would have had to worry along with the same old faces on the cheese board this year . . . Cheshire cheese in its three manifestations—red, white, and blue—is said to be the oldest of all English cheese, and the blue of the species is unquestionably the best. Its high cream content, we note with some satisfaction, makes it unsuitable for consumption by either peevish dyspeptics or people on reducing diets; just that much more for the worthy, we say."

Passing over this without comment, let us now pick up the *Catholic Worker* and read a few snatches at random:

"A neighborhood store frequently donates bags and bags of thick pretzels. No one in the house cares for them. The men on our coffee and soup lines share our distaste for these twisted gifts. Beer is the only thing which will make the pretzels a going product but this is about the last place on the face of the earth where you could serve this beverage unless you intended to close up the house. . . .

"In answer to our Fall appeal, a wounded war veteran of World War II brought in a fine warm blanket. He said he was without money but gave what he could, the blanket. On his way out he apologized to Smokey Joe for not being a pacifist. Joe told him not to feel bad. . . .

"On two different occasions I had the weird sensation of

watching a heavy-set blonde girl hammer a man on to the sidewalk along the bowery. It was a different man each time. A bystander informed me that she only begins to slam the men against the sidewalk when she is drinking. Otherwise, she is generally attempting to turn the men to religion. . . .

"As we surveyed our Thanksgiving meal we noticed the little things that were missing. There were no tablecloths nor saucers for the cups. However, I'm sure we wouldn't use them if we had them. . . .

"Losing track of the number of times that Shorty Smith has been in Bellevue hospital is not hard to come by. Shorty is in again. . . .

"Late one afternoon our dining room door was opened by a one-legged man. He explained from his sitting position on the pavement that his crutches had been stolen while he was asleep on a park bench. . . ."

As I was saying, this contrast in my reading material . . . from the $18 a pound *foie gras* to the stolen crutches . . . always leaves me with a swirling head and a temporary sense of unbalance. It also seems to call for some sort of sociological comment but I am not the one to make it. All I'm saying is that I . . . in my pleasant middle-class neighborhood . . . find *both* these worlds as strange as life in Tibet.

Sex, Always Sex

It was only a small United Press release, tucked in at the bottom of a newspaper column, but the headline happened to catch my eye. It read, succinctly: "Sex Problem." What was it *this* time, I wondered, as I quickly reviewed the possibilities. Had the Drs. Rockstein and Lieberman, of New York University, now reversed their world-shaking discovery that the female housefly outlives the male housefly? Had they goofed somewhere along the line? Me, I can't tell a girl housefly from a boy one and, hence, must terminate their life spans in a most indiscriminate fashion. Couldn't the doctors, too, have become confused?

Or was this a sex problem beyond the scope of the laboratory? Were the men of New York . . . unable to tell whether a woman was coming or going in the new sack dress . . . staging a mass protest in Madison Square Garden? They might not care about the sex of houseflies but surely it was vital to recognize a woman from a sack of Idahos?

The problems of sex, although seldom novel, were infinite. *This* sex problem, though, was definitely on the novel side and I would like to quote the news release in its entirety:

"Houston, Texas. The argument that led to the fatal shooting of Stanley Webb and the arrest of Benjamin Franklin Patterson, 60, on a charge of murder, concerned the sex of the devil. Webb held to the male theory and Patterson disagreed."

Now if there is anything that I admire in a man it is the ability to feel so *strongly* about an abstract theory that he will defend that theory to the bitter end. One sees it so seldom nowadays. Hence, I couldn't help feeling that the metaphysical discussion between the Messrs. Webb and Patterson, even though it led to bloodshed, was both admirable and refreshing.

It was admirable in the sense that they didn't waste time arguing as to whether or not there *was* a devil; it was refreshing in the sense that I've never before heard anyone argue as to the devil's sex. As with the case of Miss Dorothy Parker's alligator, I never dreamed that the question . . . but of course you know *that* story? Of course. But for the benefit of some stray hermit living on the edge of the Sahara (and I have rousing good book sales among desert hermits), maybe I'd better repeat it?

It seems that some friend, with a warped sense of humor, once sent Miss Parker an alligator . . . and she, not knowing how to dispose of the creature in the white heat of the moment, hastily dumped it into her bathtub and rushed off to keep a luncheon engagement. Upon her return home, she found that her cleaning lady, in a dignified note of farewell, had given notice: "I can't work in no house with an alligator in the bathtub. I would have told you this before but did not think the subject would ever come up."

All of which goes to show that you can't count on *anything* in this uncertain world.

How, then, did this metaphysical hassle arise between the two gentlemen down in Texas? It's difficult to reconstruct the crime, since the news release is so meagre, but I think it reasonably safe to assume that the two contestants . . . Mr. Webb and Mr. Patterson . . . had been imbibing a little fire water. And one of the properties of fire water, as we well know, is that it tends to make a man soar above the mundane problems of everyday living: to invent problems that really *are* problems; suddenly to conceive very brilliant and profound convictions that simply cry aloud for expression.

But perhaps I do the Messrs. Webb and Patterson a grave injustice? Could be. After all, there *are* people in this world who can, without benefit of fire water, become intoxicated with just the richness of their own verbiage.

One of my very favorite authors, G. B. Stern, tells this on herself in her charming book *Monogram*[1]: "Usually, when interviewers happen along and sit down opposite me with

---

[1] New York, Macmillan, 1936.

an expectant air, I have to improvise like mad, and disguise my own astonishment at the unexpected fervours that come streaming out of me. I can always summon them up from nowhere by using the phrase: 'I can't help feeling very strongly about this . . .'

"And then, smoking a cigarette and looking steadily into space as though gazing down vistas of hard work, clear thinking and research in some noble cause, wait and see what it is that I can't help feeling strongly about."

On one occasion, H. G. Wells asked her opinion about something pertaining to religion and our Miss Stern, feeling that she must make herself interesting to Mr. Wells at all costs, began wildly to improvise. "Ardently I improvised a whole complicated creed and religion unlike any other creed or religion that anyone else can ever have had: gazing steadily into space, my voice shaken with passion, I must have gone on for quite a long time. When I had done myself full justice, he merely said gently: 'Tynx, you've just this minute made up all that!' "

Later, much later (see *All In Good Time*), Miss Stern became a convert to Catholicism. Did she, one wonders, make herself equally interesting to the priest who instructed her? One need not wonder. One knows, after reading her saga, that she most certainly did. And one learns, too, that the priest . . . in handling her . . . was as gentle as Mr. Wells.

Anyhow, I feel that some such scene—but without the same gentle ending!—must have transpired between Webb

and Patterson. Did Patterson deliver himself of a truly splendid discourse, proving that the devil just *had* to be female,
only to have Webb brush him aside with a rude "Oh, Horse-
feathers!"?

We don't know. But I can't help seeing Mr. Patterson as
a dyed-in-the-wool woman hater who saw all women as the
living incarnation of Beelzebub: a man who bitterly re-
sented the idea of calling so noble a thing as a ship a "she";
a man who felt it sheer blasphemy that the Church should
be called "Mother Church."

And I see (in fact, *I feel very strongly about this!*) our
Mr. Webb as a gentleman of the old school; a chivalrous
and discerning gentleman who saw all women in an angelic
light.

Unfortunately, it was Mr. Webb who got killed.

What Is This Thing Called Love?

Have you ever fallen in love at first sight? I don't mean falling in love with a rag and a bone and a hank of hair . . . *that's* relatively painless . . . but with a house? And then have you ever had this dream house evaporate into thin air? It's a shattering experience that I wouldn't wish on my worst enemy. Hence, I sincerely hope that no readers will be so crude and insensitive as to think that this is just an essay on *real estate*. Rather, it's the story of a brief and painful love affair that only another Chekhov could do justice by.

It was on a Sunday afternoon in April and my husband and I were driving home in very low and cynical spirits. We'd just been out to inspect another house that the real estate ads (with their lyrics that would put *Ode on a Grecian Urn* to shame) had lured us into believing just *might* be habitable. We still found ourselves being trapped, all unawares, by frustrated novelists . . . now writing real estate ads . . . even though we were, at long last, beginning to catch on to the professional lingo.

For instance, the expression "Tired of taking care of a big yard?" means that the house is built flush with the front sidewalk and that there isn't a blade of grass on the premises.

The expression "House neat as a pin" means that the ad writer, even with his back to the wall, can't think of another solitary thing to say for it. It's neat. Repulsive, yes, but neat.

The expression "Out-of-town owner wants action! Drastic slash in asking price!" means that it's now a tight race between the termites and the owner who's trying to unload it. *Who* will get rid of the house first? Odds strongly in favor of the termites.

And the expression "Ideal family home for growing children" means that the place is such a shambles that not even the Dead End Kids could possibly inflict any more damage. So, why *not* let your kiddies have the fun of giving it the final kick in the shins and watch London Bridge come tumbling down?

Well, we were driving home on this particular Sunday afternoon . . . and feeling that the Kremlin had nothing on the real estate agencies when it came to false glorification . . . when we saw IT.

IT was a homemade "For Sale" sign tacked onto a magnificent elm tree in front of a white clapboard house with pale pink shutters. There was a modest, retiring, and even quaint look about the place (you have already gathered it wasn't a split-level job or even a ranch-style home, I presume?) that immediately caught my fancy. Even so, we almost didn't stop. We already had a four-bedroom home and were looking for larger quarters, not smaller ones, for heaven's sake. And we were insisting on the Miracle of Miracles: a large downstairs bedroom, with adjoining lavatory, for my seventy-nine-year-old mother. At seventy-nine, she was no longer leaping up and down stairways with her old abandon.

Our initial mistake was in idling the motor and taking a good squint at the place. Mistake #2 was in driving around the block and returning for another squint. Mistake #3 was in saying: "Well, you never can tell. Appearances can be deceiving. Maybe there's *gobs* of room."

The minute I stepped into that incredibly spacious and lovely living room, zing went the strings of my heart. "Take it easy," I cautioned myself. "Remember that *your* furniture doesn't look like hers. Take away these oriental throw rugs and that yellow satin loveseat and what've you got?"

The answer still came up: "Plenty."

There was a sunny, mellow, and quietly elegant air about that room that made me think, with the deepest conviction: "Home is the sailor, home from the sea. *Here* is where I want to spend my declining years, amen." There were long French windows, with tiny balconies outside, that reached to the floor; the most beautiful marble fireplace I'd ever seen; built-in white bookcases that reached to the ceiling. Outside the bay window, at the far end of the room, was a budding pear tree.

Through an open doorway, you glimpsed a cozy little den: complete with pale yellow draperies and more built-in bookcases. MOREOVER, all the draperies and wall-to-wall carpeting all over the house were included in the asking price. AND the price seemed not unreasonable.

This vital hazard out of the way, we proceeded to troop—with bated breath and fluttering pulse—through the rest of the place. Obviously, the living room was the *pièce de résistance* (translated, the only *large* room) but who cared? You didn't need a bedroom the size of a ballroom, did you? And why need a kitchen that more than one person could squeeze into? I was the only one who did the cooking, wasn't I?

The main thing was that everything, but everything, was in wonderful condition for an older (old?) house and you could literally *feel* all the loving care and happy living that had gone into it. (Don't tell me that houses can't talk . . . they can, they can! . . . and I soon found myself patting the widow's shoulder in compassion. How dreadful, for her, that she had to move out and let me take over.) There was even, while speaking of happy living, a recreation room over the old carriage house that featured a big, if somewhat moth-eaten, pool table. True, a pool table had never occurred to me as a prime requisite for happy living but why quibble if it was handed to me?

"This is the house I want," I announced firmly, planting myself in front of the marble fireplace, and my husband didn't even kick me in the shins. (He was staring at those built-in bookcases and lusting, absolutely lusting, after all those shelves.) Besides, why play hard to get? This was IT, wasn't it?

What if we *couldn't* all fit into the breakfast room at the same time? What if there *wasn't* a single downstairs closet, and none worth mentioning upstairs? What if there *wasn't* any cross-ventilation in those cute little bedrooms with sloping ceilings? What if the basement *was* about as big as a commemorative postage stamp?

The place was loaded with Charm and I, for one, was in full accord with Mr. Blandings (buying a decrepit Connecticut farmhouse where General Gates had once stopped to water his horses) when he argued with his lawyer: "There are *some* things you must buy with your heart, not your head."

I could even fancy myself (in lieu of dull business arrangements with the bank) just *handing* the widow my heart, on a silver tray, as a down payment.

"Well, maybe we ought to at least sleep on it," mumbled my husband, like a man just coming out from a spinal anaesthesia. (*His* heart, on a silver tray, could be used as collateral.)

I cast a frantic look at the widow. "But don't you dare sell it to anyone else," I pleaded, as I reluctantly backed out the front door.

Once home, my husband . . . whose head seemed to be

clearing more rapidly than mine . . . got out a pencil and pad and drew up two columns labeled "Advantages" and "Disadvantages." For some reason or other, the "Disadvantages" column seemed to grow in leaps and bounds, quite like Jack's beanstalk, while the "Advantages" column didn't get much farther than: "Charm. Bookcases. Marble fireplace."

"But this isn't *fair!*" I cried out passionately. "You didn't even put down the pool table or the yellow draperies. And what about that pear tree outside the bay window! Look, how can you *possibly* measure Charm versus Closets?"

"Well, we can't hang our clothes on the pear tree," said my husband, not too unreasonably, and laid down his pencil with a little sigh. It was a sad little sigh and terribly final-sounding.

Right then and there, I knew that Charm had lost the day. Right then and there, my heart began slowly to break into tiny fragments. Nor has Time, that old healer, completely mended the pieces. It was, with apologies to Deborah Kerr and Cary Grant, *An Affair To Remember.*

The Sign of the Whistling Pig

In watching the late late English movies on TV, I generally count on missing one word out of three. Once you accept this percentage in loss, it's really rather fun to piece the
dialogue together as best you can; quite adds to the Scotland
Yard atmosphere of sleuthing around foggy waterfronts. And
even if you fall badly behind in your sleuthing (e.g., darting
out to the kitchen for a coke can be *fatal*), there is always
the English landscape for compensation.

Recently I saw an old movie release of *David Copperfield*
(starring the late W. C. Fields as Micawber) and I found
myself, as usual, eagerly drinking in the Olde Englande
landscape. The truth of the matter is that England has
always held a peculiar fascination for me even though I
have no illusions, whatsoever, that it would be on the exotic
side. I am all prepared, you see, for *dinginess* in the big
cities; perhaps an over-picturesqueness in the villages. Be-

sides, I am quite certain that both the weather and the food would be on the abominable side.

Just the same, the very names tease at me: Fleet Street, Soho, Lyme, Cornwall, Brighton, Hampstead Heath, Piccadilly, and all the others that I've encountered, over and over, in my reading. Not to mention my correspondence. Some of the English return addresses are so fantastic (such as "Mop's End") that I sometimes wonder if someone is pulling my leg. Why don't they have staid sensible names like . . . well, like my own address? Diamond Avenue.

Anyhow, I would rather visit England than any other spot in the world for I want to see . . . with my own eyes . . . the crooked chimney pots against the skies, the small cultivated-down-to-the-last-square-inch British gardens, the river Thames, Westminster Abbey, and the cliffs of Dover. (Buckingham Palace and the Royal Family I will pass up . . . unless, of course, they insist on an audience.) Mainly, I just want to wander through the streets of London, inhale the fog, and maybe drop in at The Sign of The Whistling Pig for chips and ale and a game of darts.

Also, I have always been very partial to the British people: both as a lump group, sight unseen, and the individuals I've met here in America. True, I still miss one word out of three . . . and find myself, like the village idiot, repeating "Beg pardon? I didn't quite catch that?" . . . but I really think I'm improving on the pick-up. If things get *too* bad,

I can always toss in some American slang and make *them* come back with the "Beg pardons." It sort of rounds out the dialogue.

I am also very fond of England's authors, such as . . . to name but a handful . . . G. K. Chesterton, Ronald Knox, Graham Greene, Caryll Houselander, Evelyn Waugh, G. B. Stern, etc. Here, with the clipped accents out of the way, there is no confusion in getting the message. At least, there's no confusion once you catch on to words like "lift" . . . "biscuits" . . . "trams" . . . "prams" . . . "Piccadilly *Circus*," etc.

In brief, I like England and its people and it therefore pains me exceedingly that the feeling isn't mutual. (The Churchills . . . Sarah and Randolph . . . got *that* across, in no uncertain terms, in recent months. I didn't even miss one word out of three!) But let us stick . . . shall we? . . . to the Man on the Street. Here we find that the average American taxpayer would just as soon have England, and her white cliffs of Dover, at the bottom of the deep blue sea. And the average Britisher apparently chokes at just the *thought* of America. For instance, I one day received a letter from an English housewife saying that I (through my essays) was the first American she had ever liked; that I had done more, in her eyes, toward establishing international good will than the United Nations. Instead of being pleased or even amused at this quite wild tribute, it merely appalled me. The first American she had ever liked, indeed! Did she, by any chance, think that Barbara Hutton was an average American housewife?

Anyhow, I voiced this complaint . . . based on my wounded feelings as an American citizen! . . . to a British priest on the Notre Dame campus. "Cheer up!" quoth he. "I get that sort of thing *all* the time. People are forever coming up to me and saying, "I can't stand you bloody Englishmen but . . . well, now, *you're* not such a bad chap." Another Englishman tried to cheer me up by saying that the French people really hated us far more than did the British.

No one likes to be disliked for no particular good reason— either as a nation or as an individual—and I see the United States (brimming over with bumbling good will and generosity and a *desire* to be liked) being slapped down like a shop girl trying to make the Junior League. But leaving the bigger issues (political and economical) aside, what is the *basic* reason for this mutual antipathy? What personal reasons?

Elizabeth Sewell, an English writer who has been teaching in America and who, incidentally, is a Catholic convert, had this to say in an article entitled "The Death Of The Imagination"[1]:

"The English system turns us, as Newman points out, 'into beings who are proud, bashful, and reserved.' The American system produces the apparent contrary, beings who are externally self-confident, ready to rush in anywhere,

[1] Published in *Thought,* 1953.

hail-fellow-well-met, worshipping youthfulness. It is our apparent oppositeness which makes us so often intensely irritating to one another."

She then goes on to say that, despite this irritation, we are drawn to each other by a common need and that our real meeting ground is a great vacuum of intellectual and spiritual resourcelessness.

"The United States sends us Hollywood movies, nearly all our popular songs, jazz and musicals, types of television programs and styles of advertising. We send the United States our best ballet and Shakespearian companies . . . and the Royal Family news and the Coronation. Put in more general terms, America sends us her own concept of Romantic Love, as false to reality as it is to the truths of mind and heart; and we export to America relics of a splendor which was once a living part of our national existence but is now little more than a carefully preserved artificiality, and as foreign as America's product to genuine feeling and thinking."

It's quite a dismal picture—America and England throwing each other life-savers made out of cellophane!—but I give it to you for whatever it's worth. Offhand, it rather looks as if *neither* country can well afford to sneer at the other's present-day culture and spiritual resources. They have their "Teddy Boys," we have our "Juvenile Delinquents"; they have their "Angry Young Men," we have our "Beat Generation." *Quo vadis,* England? *Quo vadis,* America?

Only, would it help *my* cause any if I (although an American who has central heating and says "Gee" instead of "Coo") were to tell you about my doorstop? It's a tailor's iron, weighing several tons (give or take a little), that was brought over from England by *my British great-grandfather*. Does that help at all?

Anyhow, I'm not going to be like the small child who sulks: "If you won't like me, I won't like you. SO THERE!" I still like the British and I still want . . . someday, somehow . . . to wander through the foggy smoggy streets of London.

Nag, Nag, Nag

For some reason or other, people don't always pay close attention to what I say. I'm sure I enunciate clearly enough . . . for I can hear my own voice ringing out as clear and true as a bell . . . but the *message* doesn't seem to get through the lines. Nothing happens. I might just as well have been standing on a lonely hilltop, reading aloud from the yellow pages in the phone book, and amusing a few stray crows.

Even my *best* suggestions for bettering the world fall on such stony ground that I sometimes wonder if it's worth the effort. Then, after a brief sulking period, I brighten. I remember that Rome wasn't built in a day; that undoubtedly some woman, behind the scenes, must have done a *lot* of nagging to get those first blocks laid.

So, I thought it might not be a bad idea . . . not a bad idea at all . . . if I were to reproduce a talk that I once delivered to the priest editors of the country. Maybe they

didn't hear me so well the first time? Maybe the micro-
phone was faulty or something?

The thing is, they not only *asked* me to give this talk—at
one of the annual Catholic Press Association conventions—
but they even handed me a ready-made title: "Do Priest
Editors Underestimate the Power of a Woman?" (Already,
you can see that they sure underestimated at least *one* thing:
the womanly power to nag, nag, nag.) Well, perhaps they
were just baiting me with that provocative title . . . just
asking me to stick my neck out . . . but I, against my better
judgment, decided to oblige. After all, what did I—except
for my neck, my reputation, and my bread and butter—have
to lose?

"It seems to me," I started out, "that if priests want to
appeal more to the female trade (and I understand that
women account for 80% or more of all subscriptions received
by Catholic publications) the solution is an obvious one.
Just put out a *better* all-around magazine and pretend that
their 80% women readers are as smart as their 20% male
readers. And the obvious way to improve the quality of a
magazine would be to let more women take over. Surely,
there must be *some* women with as much native ability as,
say, the newly-ordained young priest whose Superior has
just announced, out of a clear blue sky: 'Starting next Wednesday, my boy, you're to be an editor. I understand you
once wrote an excellent paper, back in the seminary, on the
origin of Mother's Day.'

"Now I'm not suggesting women on the staff *just* to provide the Catholic woman's viewpoint (although heaven knows it's needed) but to jack up the entire magazine. It is my modest conviction that the female mind is more coldly practical and yet, at the same time, more imaginative than the male's. Also, the same patience and burning zeal for perfection that prompt a woman to shove a piece of furniture all over the house, in order to see where it looks best, might make for some interesting innovations in magazine lay-out. And have you ever watched a woman . . . with just a microscopic shred of applegreen cloth and a spool of lemon yellow thread for guidance . . . get the painters to mix *just* the colors she wants for the breakfast room? They (the painters) may know moments of dark despair . . . even threaten to walk out on the job . . . but does the little woman give up? Not she.

"I can see, of course, that this trusting a woman in the editorial field would call for great acts of faith, and even abandonment, on the part of the priests. But to paraphrase Péguy, in his poem on abandonment, I might put it this way:

> You might perhaps, and no harm
> done, leave your business in a
> woman's hands, O wise men.
> You might perhaps leave it to her
> for the space of a night

And next morning you might find
it not too badly damaged.

"I think it stands to reason that a priest editor who has
known only one woman, his mother, could well use a woman
to judge what manuscripts other women (those 80%ers)
would like. Also, a woman would be very helpful in suggesting interesting topics that the editor, in turn, could
assign to certain writers. From some of the threadbare topics
that have been handed *me*, I'd say the priests were scraping
the bottom of the barrel.

"I am convinced that women, on the whole, like strong
and vital writing. And I think one reason they don't get their
money's worth, in some of the Catholic publications, is because priests underestimate their perception, their common
sense, and their ability to catch a joke. Priests seem to be
in deadly fear that women are going to be disedified by a
frank approach to vital issues or that they're going to mis-
interpret anything that borders on the flippant or radical or
satirical side. I know this to be true because some of my
choicest passages, in an accepted manuscript, have been
removed by nervous editors. Hence, when I was compiling
my essays for book form, one of the greatest pleasures of
my life was in putting back the passages that the nervous
editors had taken out.

"Now I can think of two reasons why editors get nervous.

One is that they tend to judge their feminine readers by the crackpot letters they receive. The sad part about this is that the crackpots, who represent a distinct minority, are FOREVER writing letters to editors while the intelligent readers, on the whole, keep mum. But why must one cater to crackpots? (As if I didn't know. A subscription is a subscription is a subscription. . . .)

"Another thing that makes editors nervous is the editorial policy that seems to overshadow all Catholic publications. Maybe, for all I know, it's part of Canon Law? Anyhow, it goes like this: 'In expressing ourselves on important matters, it does not suffice to be clear enough to be understood: we must be so clear that we cannot possibly be misunderstood.'

"Well, this is an admirable principle along some lines ('No, water does NOT break the Eucharistic fast. Yes, it can be tap water, spring water, melted snow, or sea water. No, you cannot *possibly* overdrink,' etcetera) but it would be fatal to apply this to all types of writing. It would be the death knell, for instance, for a humorous essay. You couldn't stop, every three minutes, and erect signs along the way: *Just kidding. . . . Slight exaggeration here. . . . This is irony. . . . This is a clean joke. Don't be afraid to laugh. . . .*

"Nor do I think it necessary to be so careful. Whenever I speak before a group of women . . . why, you'd be surprised how intelligent they appear. I mean, they clap their hands at the right spots; are properly solemn at the right spots; and even laugh at the right spots. Much of this may be pure politeness, of course, but the important thing is that they know where the right spots *are.*

"Also, this principle of never running the risk of being misunderstood can mean that the reader, overcome by boredom, may never get past the first four paragraphs. You see, he has already grasped a few basic principles of his faith . . . such as the idea that marriage is for keeps . . . and it's rather rough on Constant Reader to plow through the same old stuff before hitting the jackpot: something *fresh* on the subject of matrimony.

"So it would be just fine with me if priest editors would get over their nervous apprehension, as regards the limitations of the female mind, and just get on with their jobs: turning out the best magazine possible, with no anxious eye on the reader's I. Q. Look what happened to the movies when *they* decided to cater to a twelve-year-old level! They hit their target, all right, but no one came out the winner."

Mostly Prejudice

I have just finished reading, for the first time in my life, the classic *Pride and Prejudice* by Jane Austen. To admit this in cold print is pretty humiliating—somewhat on a par with admitting "I've just found out who is meant by the Bard of Avon" or "I've just found out what *à la carte* stands for"—but I trust this public confession of mine will not go unrewarded: that one's guardian angel *does* give good marks for honesty. And the honest truth, I guess, is that both Grandma Moses and I are rather late starters.

Naturally, I'd always intended to get around to Jane Austen someday. "I really *must* read Jane Austen," I kept telling myself, but I felt the same urgency, the same eager anticipation, that I might feel in thinking, "Someday, I *must* have this wisdom tooth pulled."

The main reason I was gun-shy was that I had already been exposed to Jane in my green years—as witness a battered old copy of *Emma*, with "Lu Hardman, Milwaukee-Downer College" on the flyleaf, that's still around the house somewhere—and the exposure had not been too happy. I had read *Emma* with all the keen relish with which I had read *Silas Marner* and *The Last of the Mohicans*—i.e., no relish whatsoever—for I'm afraid my taste in novels, at that time, ran along more lively lines. (Yet, oddly enough, I do remember enjoying essays by Stevenson, Thoreau, and Emerson. There's no accounting, I guess, for our blind spots and our receptive spots but perhaps I just felt, not unreasonably, that novels were supposed to be entertaining. Not punishment.)

Anyhow, *Emma* had left me practically semi-conscious from boredom. People didn't really act and talk in such a stilted and ridiculous fashion or—if they really *had*, back in the early eighteen hundreds—wasn't it better just to forget the whole thing? And as to Jane Austen's idea of a rip-roaring plot . . . holy cow, no one could get *me* excited about a boy-meets-girl theme when it took boy and girl at least six chapters even to discover that they both enjoyed charades. (A passionate discovery that, oddly enough, might lead to a proposal in the next chapter. One can only regret that there were no pre-Cana Conferences in Jane Austen's day to offer a better foundation for holy wedlock.) Can you imagine any youth of today—his eyes ablaze with passion—exclaiming: "You . . . you like Chinese checkers? Oh, my darling . . . my sweet one . . . why had you never told me before? *When* can we be married? Tuesday?"

No, Jane simply wasn't the girl for me, but the distressing thing about it all was that she was forever being thrown in my face. All my favorite authors seemed to worship at the shrine of La Austen and, in my nastier moods, I wondered if they *really* liked the old girl or were just being precious. Moreover, all their chummy references to various Austen characters were nothing short of maddening. If you didn't catch on, and I surely didn't, you were clearly banished to the Siberia of Nitwits: sitting out in the cold while *other* people were laughing and chatting around the nice cozy hearth of literacy. Not to know Jane Austen, forward and backwards and sidewise, was apparently as grievous a sin— at least in literary circles—as never having heard of the Mad Hatter or Peter Pan or Tom Thumb.

Finally, I could take no more. I was fed up to the teeth with people who claimed that, if the house was burning, they would first rescue their six precious, well-thumbed novels by Jane Austen; people who, if asked what books they'd want if stranded on a desert island, would invariably start out thoughtfully: "Well, all of Jane, of course . . . and then, oh, maybe the *New Testament?*"

I had even heard, from an unimpeachable source, that a Britisher had written in to one of England's weeklies, during the blitz, and claimed to be the only man ever to be bombed off a lavatory seat while reading Jane Austen. But whether he was ever publicly decorated for this, I wouldn't know.

"I give up," I said to my husband. "I'm going to read *Pride and Prejudice* even if it kills me."

That it did not kill me, or even impair my general health, goes without saying. It's really eating worms, though, to

admit that I enjoyed it hugely . . . and greater praise has no
man (not even the one in the bombed lavatory) when you
consider the sizeable antipathy I had worked up toward
England's loved one.

I think, though, that if Jane's devotees had stressed her
deadly sarcasm—rather than how "adorably playful" she was
as a writer—I might have faced her sooner. And had I realized that most of her characters were utter fools—Mr. Collins,
for instance, is the most pompous jackass I've ever encountered in print—and that Jane *knew* they were fools, I would
have rushed out to meet her with open arms.

Along with my honest, albeit delayed by several decades,
appreciation of Miss Austen, I must frankly admit that it's
a great relief to know that I have passed the acid test. I
read her, I liked her, I'm IN! Indeed, I feel almost as proud
of my new literary rating as I am of my recently acquired
taste for broccoli.

Best of all, I am no longer sitting out in the cold. Shortly
after reading the book, I was able to smile knowingly at a
little verse by Helen Bevington in *The New Yorker* that
started out:

> " 'Marriage is a great improver,'
> Wrote Miss Jane Austen, who was
>   moved
> By the connubial bliss about her
> To stay forever unimproved."

Birds of a Feather

It is true that many a criminal goes scot-free in this imperfect world of ours but, more often than not, our sins *do* come home to roost. I know, because one of my besetting sins winged homeward shortly after the publication of *The Mouse Hunter*.

It seems that on page 133 I was guilty of . . . well, "slander" is a vicious word, and far harsher than the occasion warrants, and yet "overstatement" seems a little weak. Perhaps I can best define my sin (not to be confused with the perfume of the same name) by demonstrating what it is *not*.

Have you ever watched a man trying to tell a little anecdote to a group of friends . . . a very harmless little anecdote of no importance . . . only to have his little helpmate of a wife interrupt him, every few words, with a very literal and scrupulously honest correction? The scene, and it's one that can bring tears to the most hardened eye, goes something like this:

Husband: "You know, that reminds me of something rather

amusing that happened last Sunday. We were out taking a drive and. . . ."

Wife: "Not *last* Sunday, dear. It was Sunday before last because I distinctly remember we were over at Mother's last Sunday. You know"—(and this in an aside to the others) —"Mother hasn't been at *all* well since her gall bladder operation last June and I'm not the *least* bit satisfied with the way . . . oh, I'm sorry, dear. You go ahead and finish your little story."

Husband: "Well, we were driving along the Old Pike Road, see, and suddenly we saw this little. . . ."

Wife: "No, dear, we had just turned *off* the Old Pike Road. We had just rounded the corner and were on Mayflower Road . . . oh, I'd say about ten yards from that new filling station . . . when we suddenly saw this little boy who . . . but you go ahead, dear, and finish the story. You can tell it lots better than I."

Husband (grimly): "Well, here was this little boy, around three years old, and he was wearing this crazy. . . ."

Wife: "Oh, *no*, dear. He must have been more than *three* years. I'd say he was all of four . . . wouldn't you, dear, honestly now? . . . because I remember thinking . . . HENRY! What a dreadful thing to say to me! I was only trying to set you straight, dear. Didn't want you to *spoil* your little story."

Let it be said, in the understatement of the year, that I —in telling a story—don't let the fine details slow me down.

If an incident is of small import, I just try to get over the general rough idea and let the chips fall where they may.

In this particular case (The Case of Page 133), it seems that I . . . in describing the hazards of public speaking . . . had written this: "Sometimes it takes only a small declarative sentence to undermine a speaker's aplomb. Such as, for example, the lady in Kalamazoo who rushed up to me just as I was walking into the auditorium of Nazareth College. 'Are you *really* Lucile Hasley?' she cried out in a loud voice. 'But I thought you'd be taller and have a more aristocratic nose!' The genuine distress in her voice left me shaken to the roots. . . .," etcetera.

Hence, it was somewhat unnerving to receive a letter from the lady in question (whom I'd long since forgotten) just two days before I was to *again* speak at Nazareth. She started out, "I was reading your book, and chuckling appreciatively, when I reached the middle of page 133. There I was electrified to see my own words leap out at me. When my vision cleared, I read the paragraph again. Then I went into the bathroom and was violently and noisily ill. This is not my usual reaction to your writing but I happen to be pregnant and my stomach is easily upset."

At this point, my stomach wasn't feeling too good either. Only not for the same reason. I was wondering about libel suits and just *what* they did to writers who were unable to make a financial restitution. Ninety days in the clink? Or did you work it out via manual labor: clearing swamps, digging ditches, laying sewer pipes? It would be rough on the family, of course . . . having Mother on a road gang . . . but maybe, with good behavior, I could be home in time for Christmas?

But before I got out my pickax, and said goodbye to everyone, maybe I'd better finish the lady's letter?

I had, the lady from Kalamazoo went on to say, grossly exaggerated the situation. The truth of the matter, she said, was that she had merely observed . . . *in quiet, well-modulated tones* . . . that she had expected me to be taller and have a more aristocratic nose.

After much pondering, I decided that the crux of the matter was that she had not yelled this in a loud voice . . . it only sounded that way to *me* . . . and I am most happy, at this point, to make public acknowledgment of same. I would also like to add that the lady from Kalamazoo, she of the quiet and well-modulated tones, proved herself the perfect hostess. To put me at my ease, before I again had to face her at Kalamazoo, she graciously concluded her letter with this:

"Looking back over this letter, I realize that I exaggerate myself once in awhile to make a story sound better. Mrs. Hasley, I didn't *really* become sick to my stomach when I read page 133. It actually happened earlier in the day when my six-year-old brought in a very dead squirrel for me to prepare for burial."

Pax vobiscum, lady. I have no purple stole around my

neck but may my *pax* tide you over until Saturday night confessions.

Yet while confession like this is always good for the soul, something tells me that the Lady from Kalamazoo and the Lady from South Bend are birds of a feather and, as such, are probably past redeeming. To their dying day, they will go on saying things like "I've asked my husband a *million* times to fix that cupboard!" when—by actual count on an adding machine—it was really only 999,000 times.

My Heart's a Violin

One day, as I was indulging in some light . . . and I *do* mean light . . . reading at the hairdresser's, I came across this rewarding bit: "When Barbara Stanwyck is in the dumps, she makes trans-Atlantic phone calls to the Monseigneul Café in Paris and gets Roger Baurieux and his seventeen fiddle players to play 'My Heart's a Violin' for her."

Miss Stanwyck's simple ingenuity is getting rid of the blues left me steeped in admiration. Less imaginative women just went out and bought a pair of alligator shoes, tried out a new hair rinse, or rearranged the living room furniture. Still other women, according to medical authorities, fled to the refrigerator for comfort. I also once read about a woman who rigged up a swing in her basement and, whenever she was feeling depressed, would have herself a nice soothing swing between the furnace and the laundry tubs.

But for those women who find no relief in such simple measures . . . and who really can't afford a trans-Atlantic call to Paris . . . I do have one other remedy to offer: the writing of Father Considine. Naturally, he's a pretty poor substitute for seventeen fiddle players strumming "My Heart's a Violin" . . . if you happen to be in *that* sort of mood . . . but he's pretty wonderful in handling the spiritual blues. I mean, when you get those "Oh God, I'm a stinker and might as well lie down and quit" sort of blues.

Father Considine's special talent as a spiritual medicine man lies in the fact that he doesn't go in for long-winded harangues or metaphysical flights that drown, rather than revive, the troubled spirit. He just presents the ABC of the spiritual life in a natural and matter of fact way, much as if he were giving a weather report, and lets you carry on for yourself. No diagrams, no edifying digressions, no fancy imagery. Moreover, he seems to be a sort of Johnny-One-Note: concentrating on healing the soul, rather than active surgery. That is, he seems to stress those spiritual facts that we all want so much to believe but which, when our morale is at a low ebb, seem almost *too* good to be true.

Here, then, are some sample statements from his little booklet entitled *Delight in the Lord*:

"God does not say to the Prodigal: After some time, if I see that you really do keep your resolutions, I may reinstate you in my favor."

"God does not *endure* us. He loves us passionately,

if I may use such a word . . . more than we can understand."

"St. Mary Magdalen understood so well how to deal with Our Lord with her holy audacity. Forgiven sin is absolutely no bar to the closest union with Our Lord. It is only another claim on His love."

"It is not wrong to want sympathy and help from others in sorrow. Our Lord went to His Apostles for sympathy in His agony and He broke down and cried before them. Of course, the best sympathy comes from God, and He is the only one who can really and effectively help us."

"God made your mind, and He knows quite well its limitations. He means prayer to be our joy, not our mortification."

"God does not want our spiritual life to be a constant stress, uneasy, foggy, stormy. He loves peace and joy and spiritual gaiety. We often offend other people without meaning to do so. But God knows us through and through and understands what we mean. We can never offend Him unless we *want* to offend Him."

"You need not be always imploring God to come back to you. He can see into your heart that you want Him. Do you think you will be giving Him any information?"

"We ought to ask for great graces, not only for little ones, but for the whole world: broaden and deepen our prayers. When we are addressing God, who is infinitely rich, why ask for sixpence?"

"You are too jerky in the spiritual life; you go by fits and starts. As you get nearer to God you will go as fast, but more steadily. You have plenty of time—indeed, time does not count with God. He can give you in one moment enough graces to make you a saint. When you love a person you don't go by starts—loving him in the morning and disliking him in the afternoon. You must have the same confidence in God."

Now that's a powerful lot of quoting. I suppose I should, by rights, be hanging my head in shame . . . letting Father Considine do all the work, not me . . . but my head remains upright. It's *worth* quoting in great chunks, especially in this Age of Anxiety, and I'm sure that Fr. Considine . . . now in Heaven . . . won't feel I'm poaching on his territory. The thing is, have you ever read anything more beautifully geared to the "fits and starts" female race? Women, on the whole, need to be calmed down; coaxed into maintaining an even, steady canter that won't wind them. Men, on the whole, need someone to give them a hot-foot; someone to get them started in the *first* place.

Now generalizations are usually wild and these, no doubt, are no exception. What I mean to say is that women, by nature, are more "religious minded" than men. They can get more gummed up, too.

Anyhow, if you're the type who is only irritated by corny mottoes like "Sitting down and whining never helps a bit, Best way to get there is by keeping up your grit," then I think Father Considine is your man. He is blunt but never corny. For example, and I swear this will be my last quote, are you the sort that zig-zags back and forth, never quite able to decide what *is* God's Will? Listen: "Simply *want* to do it and it is done. Don't be like the ass who died of hunger between two bundles of hay because it did not know which to eat first. Go ahead.'"

Yes, and now you might go ahead and order some of his pamphlets from the National Shrine of Our Lady of La Salette, Ipswich, Mass. And which bale of hay should you choose? Well, you might start out with his classic *Words of Encouragement*. Best of all, none of these pamphlets, which are published in England, cost over twenty-five cents. Much, *much* cheaper than putting in a call to Paris when you're in the dumps.

There is also a far graver issue at stake.

We are living in a very critical age. Indeed, as I write this, a great pall has fallen over the nation. The women are disappearing into sack dresses, with scarcely a bubble to mark the spot, and their husbands are stomping the ground and yelling to high heaven. Among the more articulate yellers is columnist Robert Ruark who somberly warns that Madame is in for some real trouble with the menfolk. "There is no doubt," he says, "that the sack, chemise, or old bag . . . call it what you will . . . is the most repulsive piece of dry-goods that these silly chicks have ever allowed themselves to be conned into."

How this Cold War will resolve itself, I wouldn't know,

but I can read the danger signals. All men, says Thoreau, lead lives of quiet desperation . . . but this doesn't sound as if it's going to be very quiet, does it?

My message, then, to the women of America . . . and I'm quite sure Father Considine would go along with me . . . is simply this:

Even if Paris *has* decreed that we drape ourselves in these sad sack dresses, let's watch out that we don't become spiritual sad sacks as well. I honestly don't think our husbands could stand us both ways.